PROMOTING READING WITH READING PROGRAMS

A How-To-Do-It Manual

ROBIN WORKS

HOW-TO-DO-IT MANUALS FOR
SCHOOL AND PUBLIC LIBRARIANS
Number 9

Series Editor: Barbara L. Stein

NEAL-SCHUMAN PUBLISHERS, INC.
New York, London

Published by Neal-Schuman Publishers, Inc.
100 Varick Street
New York, NY 10013

Library of Congress Cataloging-in-Publication Data

Works, Robin
    Promoting reading with reading programs : a how-to-do-it manual /
Robin Works.
       p.   cm. — (How-to-do-it manuals for school and public
librarians ; no. 9
    Includes bibliographical references and index.
    ISBN 1-55570-115-9
    1. Libraries, Children's—United States—Activity programs.
2. School libraries—United States—Activity programs.   3. Reading
4. Children—United States—Books and reading.   I. Title.
II. Series.
Z718.3.W67   1992
027.62′5—dc20

CONTENTS

SERIES EDITOR'S PREFACE

School library media specialists are vitally involved in the reading process. Public librarians also realize the urgency of promoting reading among their young library patrons. With the help of this volume in the *How-To-Do-It Manuals for School and Public Librarians* series, their job will be made easier and more fun! *Promoting Reading With Reading Programs* is filled with practical and interesting ideas for using books with children of all ages. It combines new literature with traditional literature, incorporating many different techniques for promoting reading into a usable whole.

The introduction helps librarians with the practical aspects of planning and promoting reading programs and activities in their libraries. Also included is a special section on promoting reading to hearing-impaired children.

The next four chapters are the outlines for programs that promote reading. These program ideas are conveniently divided by age level. They are also planned around various themes that are all related to the titles of each chapter. Ideas using everything from rocks to puppets to carrots are included.

In the margins by certain activities, you will note small illustrations. These are keyed to the full-size pattern appendix at the end of the book, making it easy to match the pattern to the activity.

Chapter 5 examines publicity and promotion. Included are ideas for budget planning, writing press releases and letters, and displays. Another helpful feature of *Promoting Reading With Reading Programs* is the annotated bibliography and filmography of selected titles from the text.

The author brings together her many years of experience in working with children. She shares her talents for creative activities and illustrations, providing many patterns for your use. Whether your library is small or large, there will be useful ideas for you in this volume of the How-To-Do-It series.

Barbara L. Stein
Series Editor

INTRODUCTION

Welcome to *Promoting Reading With Reading Programs*. This How-To-Do-It Manual not only includes useful literature based activities, but also ideas for publicity, displays, community networking, and resource sharing to help promote reading in your library. Using this manual you should be able to plan and execute successful reading programs, which can be done individually or as a series. Also included are instructions for developing a reading club where children keep track of the books they read or the time they spend reading.

STRUCTURE

Each chapter has a theme that might be used for a week or a month of your reading program. The sections are subdivided by program and age level. In each section there are themes, ideas and books for programs for Preschool through Grade Two and Grades Three and up. The themes are used to tie the literature presented into a memorable whole. Themes will also help with planning, and challenge you to look for new and different materials to use. In each chapter, there are programs with the following structures:

Preschool through Grade Two: 30 minute storytimes that includes books, films, and various literature extension activities such as fingerplays, dramatics, puppets, crafts, etc.

Grades Three through Seven: 30 minute to 1 hour programs that include booktalks, a film or guest speaker, or some additional activity such as creative writing, drama, or art.

USING AUDIO VISUAL MATERIALS

When should you use films and videos?

Although it is always preferable to use a book in storytime, many librarians use films to supplement their programs. Some suggestions for very good films are included when they would enhance a program.

PATTERNS 1 and 1a

Nametags

When you are trying to decide whether or not to use a film or video, ask yourself these questions:

- Is it necessary to use a film or video format because the book has small or very detailed illustrations that cannot be used with a group of children?
- In the case of a wordless picture book, does adapting it for film or video enhance its use with a group of children?
- Does the translation to film/video enhance the effect and meaning of the story in some way?

(Reprinted from *On Beyond Reading: Summer Reading Program 1989*, North Carolina Division of Cultural Resources, North Carolina State Library, 1989.)

If you want more information on choosing good videos, contact your local state library to see if they have the video *Choosing the Best in Children's Video*, ALA, 1990.

IDEA STARTERS

These program ideas are only a springboard, meant to be used in a flexible manner and combined creatively. Use them in ways that best fit the structure of your program depending on your community and philosophy. You may choose to organize your activities loosely, or have them more formally structured. Either style of programming can be successful if you keep your audience in mind. Try to be flexible in your approach, so all the children who want to participate can do so. Care should be taken not to accidentally exclude certain children, for example, children with reading difficulties, children with disabilities, or the child who can attend for only part of the summer.

Because of limited space, only a small number of books is listed with each program. There are lots of other wonderful titles that are not listed, so use your own favorites with the activity ideas. There are old favorites as well as new stories listed. Let your imagination soar as you choose addititonal materials to use. Some good tools to use in finding other titles are *A to Zoo, Fantasy Literature for Children and Young Adults,* and the *Juniorplots* series.

PATTERNS 2 and 2a

Nametags

PATTERNS 3 and 3a

Nametags

Things to think about

Nametags: Will help you get to know the names of the children as well as help give them a sense of identity. Some nametag ideas are included in the pattern appendix. (Patterns 1-3) Give the nametags out when you register children for your programs or maybe even every week.

Bulletin Boards: Are an excellent way to advertise your programs. Lots of questions get asked about large, catchy bulletin boards and some bulletin board ideas are included in the chapters.

Community Resources: Provide excellent opportunities to use guests and experts from your community. This makes sense not only from a programming standpoint, but also generates positive publicity within the organizations from which volunteers come.

PLANNING

Use this checklist as you plan your reading clubs.

- What age groups do you want to attract for these activities?
- Decide the days, times, and length of programs. Check city and social calendars for conflicts.
- Decide if and when registration will be held.
- Find out deadlines for school and community newspapers, church bulletins, and radio or TV programs.
- Decide when to make school visits and make the necessary arrangements. Consider making a video introduction for the basics of the reading club.
- Make sure everyone on your library's staff is aware of the summer programs schedule and events.
- Will there be a special opening or closing event for your programs? What and when?

(Adapted from *Summer Reading Program Planning Kit*, Colorado Department of Education, State Library and Adult Education Office, 1990.)

Use a time line to help you organize and plan your program. The following is adapted from *A Librarian's Planning Hand-*

TIP FOR PUBLIC LIBRARIANS
Contact area schools and learn about school visitation procedures four months ahead of time.

book for the Texas Reading Club, by Jody Phelan. (Texas State Library, 1986)

Four Months Before

- Design goals and objectives.
- Determine strategies for all objectives and identify dates for each.
- Determine length of program series in weeks.
- List ideas for potential programs.
- Evaluate community resources in light of program ideas.
- Evaluate library resources in light of program ideas.
- Initiate community resource file and design procedure to keep it current.
- Investigate vehicles for program publicity.
- Evaluate library collection of book and non-book materials and order needed materials immediately.

Three Months Before

- Draft rules/ regulations for reading club participation.
- Outline publicity schedule.
- Design in-house procedures for handling reading club activities.
- Order additional office and other supplies to support reading club activities.
- Select activities and programs from the list you compiled.
- Choose the ones that your library can sponsor.
- Identify costs for each program/activity.
- Draft tentative schedule of programs.
- Select tentative dates for beginning and end of reading club programs.
- Make preliminary investigation of presentor availability and costs for programs.
- Begin an informal in-house publicity campaign by mentioning programs to children, parents, volunteers, faculty/staff, and others.
- Draft programming budget.
- Solicit items/money from businesses, individuals, or other organizations.

WORKSHEET 1

PROGRAM COSTS: INDIVIDUAL PROGRAM

Presentor Fee or Gift

Rental Fee

>Equipment

>AV Equipment

>Space

>Presentor Requested Items

Supplies

>Arts and Crafts Items

>Take-Home "Goodies"

>Plates, Cups, Napkins, for Refreshments

Refreshments

Copyright Fees

Publicity

>In-House

>Community Wide

Additional Staff

Stationary, Postage

Overhead Costs (If program is held after hours, cost of staff, room, etc.)

Additional Insurance

Misc.

Subtotal _____

Less Donations _____

TOTAL COST _____

WORKSHEET 2

PROGRAM COSTS: SERIES

Total Costs for Individual Programs

Program 1

Program 2

Program 3

Program 4

Program 5

Program 6

Program 7

Program 8

Program 9

Program 10

Additional Staff for Series

Additions to Library Collection

   for Programming Efforts

Production Costs (Art & Printing)

Bookmarks

Posters

Flyers

Buttons

Misc.

Stationary, Postage

Subtotal _____

Less Donations _____

Total Series Cost _____

**TIP FOR PUBLIC
LIBRARIANS**
Two months before the program
starts, finalize dates for school
visits.

• Contact local cable, radio, and television stations, newspapers, and other organizations to learn procedures for publicizing your events.

Two Months Before

• Finalize dates of reading club and programs. Make news releases available for all organizations for inclusion in their newsletters.
• Design publicity brochures detailing the events planned for reading club activities and programs.
• Design bulletin boards and exhibits to be used throughout reading club dates.
• Refine program budget.
• Contact local radio, cable and television channels to arrange an interview to discuss your reading club and its events.
• Finalize presentor agreements to present programs.

One Month Before

• Print publicity.
• Place publicity in strategic locations throughout library and community.
• Begin aggressive publicity campaign.
• Send program information to cable stations for inclusion in cable announcement service.
• Compose and mail presentor letters.
• Decorate library with posters, streamers, bulletin boards, etc., to announce reading club programs.
• Make a list of photographable events and send to local newspapers.
• Compose and distribute public service announcements to local radio and television stations.
• Review budget and alter if necessary.
• Design a program evaluation form and duplicate.
• Meet with staff/volunteers to discuss upcoming programs.

You may also want to plan for the cost of the programs and then produce a budget for the entire reading club. Worksheets one and two are useful forms adapted from *A Librarian's Planning Handbook for the Texas Reading Club* by Jody Phelan (Texas State Library, 1986.)

SERVING THE HEARING IMPAIRED

With the passing of the Americans with Disabilities Act into law, the public has become more aware of the rights and needs of disabled persons. Libraries will, as public institutions, be making changes over the next two years to meet the legal requirements of the ADA.

One group of people with disabilities for which libraries need to improve service is the hearing impaired. A hearing impairment is an invisible disability, which sometimes causes children with this disability to be neglected in the library. Keep this in mind as you attempt to include all children in summer reading clubs and activities.

There are four steps to implementing services to hearing impaired children in your library:

1. Awareness: Become aware of who belongs to this population. Vocational/rehabilitation state agencies and schools are your primary resources. Become aware of how difficult it is for hearing impaired children to get the same services as the rest of the population because of the severity of the communication barriers.

2. Knowledge: Learn all you can about hearing impairment, deafness, and communication with the hearing impaired child.

3. Understanding: Find out how to change your library services and programs to make them accessible to the hearing impaired child.

4. Action: Take an aggressive approach to making changes happen. Take a sign language class or become your library's advocate for the hearing impaired child.

Possible services for the hearing impaired child:

- Signed storytime or interpreted storytime
- Closed captioned videos for children
- A telecaption decoder for check out by hearing impaired patrons
- Children's department staff use of sign language

Services for the parents of hearing impaired children:

- Information and referral on hearing impaired and deafness
- Bibliographies of books about hearing impaired and deafness.

Following are some sample storytime programs for the hearing impaired child, age 5 through grade 2. Stories are to be signed or simultaneously signed and read.

Theme: Curiosity

Books

- Barton, Byron. *Where's Al?* Seabury, 1972.
- Giganti, Paul. *How Many Snails? A Counting Book.* Greenwillow, 1988.
- Shaw, Charles Green. *It Looked Like Spilt Milk.* Harper and Row, 1947.
- Yekati, Niki. *What's Silly?* Clarion, 1989.
- Ziebel, Peter. *Look Closer.* Clarion, 1989.

Use as a flannel board: Martin, Bill. *Brown Bear, Brown Bear, What Do You See?* Holt, 1983. (Found in *Felt Board Fun* by Liz and Dick Wilmes, Building Blocks, 1984, pp. 104, 115-117.)

Wordless Film: *Rosie's Walk.* Weston Woods, 1970, 5 min.

Activity: Brown Bear Color Sheet (Enlarge Brown Bear from *Felt Board Fun* to color.)

Props to use: Crayons and other items in *Look Closer,* milk, snail shells to count.

Theme: Ducks

Books

- Ginsburg, Mirra. *The Chick and the Duckling.* Macmillan, 1972.

PATTERN 4

Ducky Mask

- Raffi. *Five Little Ducklings*. Crown, 1989.
- Roy, Rob. *Three Ducks Went Wandering*. Clarion, 1979.
- Tafuri, Nancy. *Have You Seen My Duckling?* Greenwillow, 1984.
- Wellington, Monica. *All My Little Ducklings*. Dutton, 1989.

Use as a flannel board: Pomerantz, Charlotte. *One Duck, Another Duck*. Greenwillow, 1984.

Wordless Film: *Ugly Duckling*. Walt Disney, 1969, 9 min.

Activity: Ducky Mask (see pattern number 4)

Props to use: Rubber ducky or stuffed duck, ducks cut from pellon to count.

Theme: On Hearing Impairments

Books:

- Ancona, George and Mary Beth. *Handtalk Zoo*. Four Winds, 1989.
- Brown, Tricia. *Someone Special, Just Like You*. Holt, Rinehart, Winston, 1982.
- Charlip, Remy; Ancona, George, and Mary Beth. *Handtalk Birthday*. Four Winds, 1987.
- Levi, Dorothy Huffman. *A Very Special Friend*. Kendall Green, 1989.
- Peterson, Jeanne Whitehouse. *I Have a Sister, My Sister is Deaf*. Harper and Row, 1984.
- Starowitz, Anne M. *The Day We Met Cindy*. Kendall Green, 1988.

Use as a flannel board: Sign language alphabet.

Wordless film: *Sign Me a Story*. Random House Home Videos, 1987. (Little Red Riding Hood)

PATTERN 5

ILY (I Love You) Puppet

Activity: ILY (I Love You) Puppets (see pattern number 5)

RESOURCES: ORGANIZATIONS

These are national organizations to which you can write for information on the hearing impaired child:

Alexander Graham Bell Association
3417 Volta Place, NW
Washington, DC 20078

American Society for Deaf Children
814 Thayer Avenue
Silver Spring, MD 20910

National Association for the Deaf
814 Thayer Avenue
Silver Spring, MD 20910

National Information Center on Deafness
Gallaudet University
800 Florida Avenue, NE
Washington, DC 20002

RESOURCES: BOOKS AND OTHER MEDIA

James Stanfield Publishing Co.
PO Box 1983
Santa Monica, CA 90640
1-800-421-6534
213-395-7466

Modern Talking Picture Service
Captioned Films for the Deaf
5000 Park Street, North
St. Petersburg, FL 33709
1-800-276-6213

Random House, Inc.
400 Hahn Road
Westminster, MD 21157
1-800-773-3000
1-800-726-0600

T.J. Publishing
817 Silver Spring Avenue, room 206
Silver Spring, MD 20910
301-585-4440
301-585-5930

RESOURCES: PERIODICALS

American Annals of the Deaf
Conference of Executives of American Schools for the Deaf
5034 Wisconsin Avenue, NW
Washington, DC 20016

Apropos
National Center on Educational Media
Materials for the Handicapped
Ohio State University
220 West 12th Avenue
Columbus, OH 43210

Deaf American
National Association for the Deaf
814 Thayer Avenue
Silver Spring, MD 20910

Early Years
Box 7414
Chicago, IL 60680

Endeavor
International Association of Parents of the Deaf
84 Thayer Avenue
Silver Spring, MD 20910

Exceptional Children
The Council for Exceptional Children
1920 Association Drive
Reston, VA 20091

Exceptional Parent
Box 101
Back Bay Annex
Boston, MA 02117

Volta Review
Alexander Graham Bell Association
3417 Volta Place, NW
Washington, DC 20078

RESOURCES: BOOKS ON SIGN LANGUAGE

Bornstein, Harry; Sauliner, Karen; Hamilton, Lillian. *The Comprehensive Signed English Dictionary.* Washington, DC: Gallaudet College Press, 1983.

Costello, E. *Signing: How to Speak With Your Hands.* New York: Bantam, 1983.

Gustason, G.; Pfetzing, D.; Zawolkow, E. *Signing Exact English.* Los Alamitos, CA: Modern Signs Press, 1980.

Hoemann, H. *Introduction to American Sign Language.* Bowling Green, OH: Bowling Green Press, 1986.

Riekeof, L. *Joy of Signing.* Springfield, MO: Gospel Publishing House, 1978.

Shroyer, E.H. *Signs of the Times.* Washington, DC: Gallaudet College Press, 1984.

RESOURCES: RECOMMENDED READING

Association of Library Service to Children, Young Adult Services Division, and Association of Specialized and Cooperative Library Agencies. *Challenge: Serving Deaf and Hearing Impaired Children and Their Parents.* (Brochure) Chicago: ALA, 1982.

Benderly, Beryl L. *Dancing Without Music: Deafness in America.* New York: Doubleday, 1980.

Bevan, Richard C. *Hearing Impaired Children: A Guide for Concerned Parents and Professionals.* Springfield, IL: Thomas Books, 1988.

Biehl, Jane. "Storyhours for the Deaf," *Ohio Media Spectrum*, 30(January 1978):43-46.

———. *Staff Sensitivity Workshop: Helping the Deaf Patron.* Canton, OH: Stark County District Library, 1984.

Dalton, Phyllis I. "Focus on Service to the Disabled," in *The ALA Yearbook, 1983.* Chicago: ALA, 1983: 69-71.

Daniles, Gladys R. "Disabilities Act Cleared," *Nation's Cities Weekly,* 13(July 16, 1990):17.

————. "Americans With Disabilities Act: How Expansions of Civil Rights Impacts Cities," *Nation's Cities Weekly,* 13(Aug. 20, 1990):1-2.

Dansky, Yona. "Services for the Deaf," *Catholic Library World,* 51:1 (July-Aug. 1979):22-23.

Dequin, Henry C. *Librarians Serving Disabled Children and Young People.* Littleton, CO: Libraries Unlimited, 1983.

Dresang, Elizabeth. "Mainstreaming All Children: Exceptional Children Use School and Public Libraries," *Wisconsin Library Bulletin,* March/April 1978:68-70.

Grant, June. *The Hearing Impaired: Birth to Six.* Boston: College-Hill, 1987.

Harris, Karen. "Selecting Library Materials for Exceptional Children," *School Media Quarterly,* 8(Fall 1979):24.

Huffman, Edythe F. *Library Services for the Deaf, Blind, and Physically Disabled in the United States, 1977-1979.* Chapel Hill, NC: University of North Carolina, 1980.

Huston, Patrick. "Storytelling," *Volta Review,* 74(Feb. 1972): 200-204.

Meadow, Kathryn P. *Deafness and Child Development.* Los Angeles: University of California Press, 1980.

Metcalf, Mary Jane. "Helping Hearing Impaired Students," *School Library Journal,* Jan. 1979:27-29.

Padden, Carol and Humphries, Tom. *Deaf in America: Voices From Another Culture.* Harvard University Press, 1988.

Parlato, Salvatore. *Films: Too Good for Words—A Dictionary of Non-Narrated Films.* New York: Bowker, 1972.

Phillipoff, Martha. "Serving the Deaf Child," *Georgia Librarian,* 14(Nov. 1977):39-40.

Quist, Janet. "Senate Clears Disability Bill," *Nation's Cities Weekly,* 12(Sept. 11, 1989):6.

Sacks, Oliver. *Seeing Voices: A Journey into the World of the Deaf.* Berkeley, CA: University of California Press, 1989.

Sangster, Collette. "Library Service for the Hearing Impaired," *The Bookmark,* 40(Fall 1981):25.

———. "Library Service for the Hearing Impaired," *The Bookmark,* 35(Winter 1979):50-63.

Simpson, Glenn. "Disabled See Hope for Civil Rights," *Insight on the News.* 57(Aug. 28, 1989):22.

Smith, Harry. "Games and Simulation Studies for the Deaf," *American Annals of the Deaf,* 124(Sept. 1979):611-615.

Velleman, Ruth A. *Serving Physically Disabled People: A Handbook for All Libraries.* New York: Bowker, 1979.

Walker, Lon A. *A Loss for Words: The Story of Deafness in the Family.* New York: Harper and Row, 1987.

RESOURCES

RESOURCES: SPEAKERS

Some possibilities for speakers to add diversity to your programs might be:

- art teachers
- pet shop owners
- authors
- puppeteers
- clowns
- storytellers
- dance teachers
- ventriloquists
- dentists
- veterinarians
- doctors
- zookeepers
- illustrators
- magicians
- musicians
- nature center personnel

RESOURCES: MUSIC

Educational Activities
Box 87
Baldwin, NY 11510
1-800-656-3739

Educational Record Center
Building 400/ Suite 400
1575 Northside Drive, NW
Atlanta, GA 30318-4298
(404) 352-8282

Kimbo Educational
10 North Third Avenue, B
Long Branch, NJ 07780
1-800-631-2187

Music For Little People
Box 1460
Redway, CA 95560
1-800-343-4445

Jazz Cat Productions
3455 McDowell Blvd. #203
Petaluma, CA 94954

RESOURCES: MISCELLANEOUS

National Wildlife Federation: 1400 16th Street, NW, Washington, DC 20036-2266 (1-800-432-6569). Nature discovery kits for $10 to $20 such as Gardening with Wildlife Kit, Naturescope's Discover Insects Kit, Sky Science Kit, and Backyard Science Kit. Kits include hands on activities for discovering their themes. Also ask for the book *Wild and Crafty*, 56 pages of animal facts with extension activities— $7.00, and Fossil Hunt Kit, $24.95, with 25 authentic fossils to find in volcanic sand.

Alyce Ruth Enterprises: RR1 Box 55, Woodbine, IA 51579, (712-647-3275). Very high quality puppets such as a crow, dragon, camel, kangaroo, lamb, whale, and unicorn. $40 to $75 and worth every penny!

Demco, Inc.: Box 7488, Madison, WI 53707, (1-800-356-1200). If you need extra posters or publicity, Demco has a "Discover Camp Library" poster, bookmark, and button kit. It is decorated with several animals in a tent. (See *American Libraries*, March 1990:265) catalog #x131-3642.

Anderson's It's Elementary: White Bear Lake, MN 55110, (1-800-328-9640). Incentives such as buttons, ribbons, pins, stickers, pencils, certificates, both custom and ready made.

RESOURCES FOR POSTERS, VIDEOS, FILMSTRIPS AND MORE

National Celebration of the Outdoors
1250 24th Street, NW
Washington, DC 20037
(202) 293-4800

Geological Society of America
3300 Penrose Place
PO Box 9140
Boulder, CO 80301
1-800-472-1988

Environmental Protection Agency
Public Information Center
401 M Street, SW
Washington, DC 20460
1-800-828-4444

Junior Great Books
Great Books Foundation
50 E. Huron St.
Chicago, IL 60611
   Write for information on the Junior Great Books Discussion groups.

Clowns of America, Inc.
POB 570
Lake Jackson, TX 77566-0570
   For information on clowns and clowning.

Earthwatch
680 Mount Auburn Street
Box 403 N
Watertown, MA 02272
   An ecological society.

Magical Youths International
61551 Bremer Highway
Mishawaka, IN 46544
   An organization for young magicians.

North American Society of Ventriloquism
800 Littleton Blvd.
POB 420
Littleton, CO 80160

National Geographic Society
Educational Services, Dept. 88
17th and N Streets
Washington, DC 20036

1 LET'S VISIT CAMP WANNA-READ

Get ready to go to Camp Wanna-Read. Your family will see you off, and your friends will be there to greet you. You will write letters, even to that pesky brother or sister you left at home! So pack up and go!

THEME: CAMP

Children love camp. Meet some of literature's favorite camp characters.

PROGRAM 1

Age Level: Ps—Grade 2

Books

- Bach, Alice. *The Most Delicious Camping Trip Ever.* Harper & Row, 1976.
- Delton, Judy. *My Mom Made Me Go to Camp.* Delacorte, 1989.
- McPhail, David. *Pig Pig Goes to Camp.* Dutton, 1983.
- Schwartz, Amy. *How I Captured a Dinosaur.* Orchard, 1988.

Opening: Introduce camp with the following song to the tune of The Farmer in the Dell:

A-camping we will go, a-camping we will go
Hi-ho the derry-o, a-camping we will go!

Other verses:

PATTERN 6

Lunch Sack Pigs

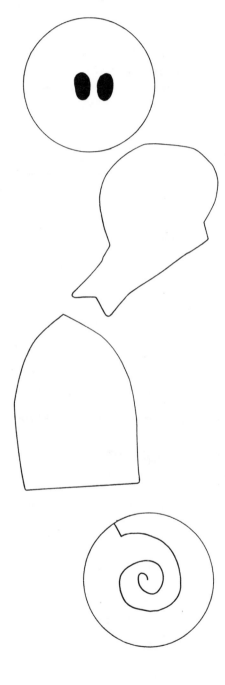

We unpack the car. . .
We build up the tent. . .
We gather wood for fire. . .
We sing a campfire song. . .
The stars are coming out. . .
We all fall asleep. . .
Pantomime the actions while singing.

Fingerplay: (To go with *Pig Pig Goes to Camp*).

Five green and speckled frogs,
Sitting on a speckled log,
Eating the most delicious bugs, YUM YUM.
One jumped into the pool,
Where it was nice and cool,
Now there are four green speckled frogs, GULP,
GULP.
(Hold up five fingers of right hand over left arm, which is the
log. Make one finger jump off your log and into an imaginary
pool. Continue singing until there are no more frogs.)

Activity: Serve trail snacks, such as raisins, granola bars, etc.

Camp Crafts: Lunch Sack Pigs. Stuff a lunch sack with scrap
paper and tape it shut. Now cut out the ears, legs, nose, and
tail patterns from pink construction paper. Glue them to the
sack. Color eyes and other details with crayons. See Pattern 6.

Camp Crafts: Sleeping bags. You Need: Construction paper,
stapler, stickers or precut shapes such as flowers, stars, or
hearts, scissors, and glue. Staple or glue two pieces of construction paper together along three sides, leaving a short end
open. Children decorate their sleeping bags and then use them
for a toy sleeping bag.

Camp Crafts: Tent: Each child needs one sheet of heavy paper.
The paper is folded into a pyramid to make an A-frame tent.
Tape the tent together and decorate. This activity can be done
with a large box such as a refrigerator box to make a lifesize
tent.

PROGRAM 2

Age Level: Grades 3 and up.

Books

- Conford, Ellen. *Hail, Hail, Camp Timberwood.* Little Brown, 1978.
- Danzinger, Paula. *There's a Bat in Bunk Five.* Delacorte, 1980.
- Landon, Lucinda. *Meg MacIntosh and the Mystery at Camp Creepy.* Joy Street Books, 1990.
- Schneider, Susan. *Please Send Junk Food.* Putnam, 1985.

Film: *Runaway Ralph.* Chuchill, 1987, 40 min.

Special Projects: Banner Brigade. Two sheets of construction paper 12 × 18-inches long, a 30-inch piece of yarn, glue crayons or markers, fabric scraps. Use one 12 × 18-inch paper for the main part of the banner. Leave a 1-inch margin at both the top and bottom. Decorate the banner to represent Camp Wanna-Read or your favorite book about camp. Other slogans can also be used, such as "Be a Happy Library Camper." Make frames for the top and bottom by cutting two 4-1/2 × 12-inch pieces of paper from the other construction paper. Fold each of these pieces twice the long way to form two 1-1/8-inch pieces. Place the yarn along the inside fold of one frame. Then glue the frame over the top of the banner with the folded flap towards the front. Glue the bottom frame in the same manner but with no yarn. Use the fabric scaps to glue decorations on your banner. Hang by the yarn. have a banner making contest with everyone getting a ribbon. Display these banners at a local mall or in the town square. If there is a parade planned in your city for the summer, then have the library kids march in it with their banners.

THEME: LETTERS TO HOME

Age Level: Grade 3—6

Craft: Make a Letters to Home Book. (See pages 162-164 of *This Way to Books* for a letters to book characters activity and mailbox exhibit. Caroline Feller Bauer, H. W. Wilson, 1986.)

PATTERN 7

Letters-To-Home Shape

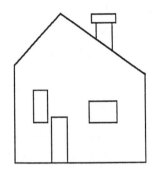

Cut two house patterns from construction paper. Staple together several sheets of white paper cut in the same house shape with the construction paper covers on them. Let children draw their families in the windows of the houses. See Pattern 7.

Books

- Cleary, Beverly. *Dear Mr. Henshaw*. ABC-Clio, 1987.
- Pfeffer, Susan Beth. *Dear Dad, Love Laurie*. Scholastic, 1989.
- Rocklin, Joanne. *Dear Baby*. Collier Macmillan, 1988.
- Va, Leong. *A Letter to the King*. HarperCollins 1991.
- VanLeeuwen, Jean. *Dear Mom, You're Ruining My Life*. Dial, 1989.

Film: *The Letter*. Films Incorporated, 1970, 5 min.

Special Project: Start a library pen pal club. Here are some places to send for information:

Friends Forever Pen Pal Club
P.O. Box 20103, Park West Post Office
New York, NY 10025
Cost: $3.00

International Pen Friends
P.O. Box 290065
Brooklyn, NY 11229-0001
Cost: SASE

Pen Pals Unlimited
P.O. Box 6283
Huntington Beach, CA 92615
Cost: $2.00 and SASE

Student Letter Exchange
Waseca, MN 56093
Cost: SASE

World Pen Pals
1690 Como Avenue
Saint Paul, MN 55108
Cost: $3.00 and SASE

Advice Column: On a large bulletin board, write the words "Dear Happy Camper." This will serve as a place to display letters written for advice in the manner of "Dear Abby" except these letters are for advice about camp. Dilemmas, signed with fictitious funny names are deposited in a box for this purpose. The librarian can post humorous answers from "Happy Camper" on the board. This activity works well with teen volunteers.

Craft: Pop-Up Card. You need 9 × 12-inch construction paper, markers or crayons, glue, colored paper scraps. Fold the construction paper in half to make a greeting card. Cut a 1 × 4-inch rectangle off the top as shown. Make a dot on the fold 3 inches from the top. Fold the tab down on that dot making the center fold parallel to the top and bottom edges. Turn the card over and crease the tab on the other side also. Open the card and you will see a triangular base with a tab on top of it. Refold along the center fold, pressing the tab and triangle inside the card. Decorate the tab with a funny face or shape. Write a greeting and mail to your pen pal! See Figure 1-1.

FIGURE 1-1 Making a Pop-Up Card

THEME: GRANDPARENTS

Kids write letters to their grandparents from camp. With this in mind, do a multigenerational library time. Send home invitations with the children inviting their grandparents to come to the library for a special session with them. Do this well in advance to give out-of-town grandparents a chance to come also.

PROGRAM 1

Age: Ps—Grade 2

Books

- Cole, Joanna. *The Trouble With Grandad.* G.P. Putnam's, 1988.
- Gray, Nigel. *A Balloon for Grandad.* Orchard, 1988.
- Johnston, Tony. *Grandpa's Song.* Dial, 1990.
- Levinson, Ricki. *I Go With My Family to Grandma's.* Dutton, 1986.
- Schwartz, Amy. *Oma and Bobo.* Bradbury, 1987.

Film: *The Napping House.* Weston Woods, 1985, 5 min.

Fingerplay:

My Grandparents went to Myrtle Beach (march in place)
And sent us back a Turtle each (cup hands and look inside)
Then they went to Katmandu (march again)
And sent us back a Cockatoo (flap arms like wings)
But the best gift that I can see (point to eyes)
Is when they are at home with me! (hug yourself)

Activity: *A Balloon for Grandad* is the perfect book to accompany a balloon launch. Each child writes a message to a grandparent and sends the balloon off. The message doesn't have to be to their own grandparent, but they may want to save the balloon for their own grandmother or grandfather.

Fingerplay: (Share the traditional action rhyme "Grandma's Glasses").

> Here are Grandma's glasses (make small glasses with hands)
> Here is Grandma's hat (make small hat with hands)
> This is the way she folds her hands and puts them in her lap.
> Here are Grandpa's glasses (make large glasses with hands)
> Here is Grandpa's hat (make large hat with hands)
> This is the way he folds his arms and sits like that!

Craft: Reading coupons to give to grandparents. You need: Construction paper, scissors, crayons, hole punch, and ribbon. Have the children design their coupons, which can be good for reading aloud to their grandparents or having their grandparents read aloud to them. If a grandparent lives out of town, suggest a poem reading over the phone, or a reading during a specific date for the coupons value. Design 3 × 6-inch coupons, then hole punch each and string them on ribbon.

PROGRAM 2

Age: Grades 3 and up

Books

- Byars, Betsy. *A Blossom Promise.* Delacorte, 1987.
- Clifford, Eth. *The Remembering Box.* Houghton Mifflin, 1985.
- Nixon, Joan Lowry. *Maggie, Too.* HBJ, 1985.
- Strauss, Linda. *The Alexandra Ingredient.* Crown, 1988.

Film: *The Electric Grandmother.* Learning Corporation of America, 1982, 34 min.

Activity: Design a family newspaper. Have the kids make a list of current events happening in their family such as births, anniversaries, lost teeth, etc. They can then write short articles to go in their papers. Have them also include drawn "related photos" for their stories. Give the newspapers appropriate names such as "The Smithville Times" or the "Jones Gazette."

Activity: Make a family recipe book. Have the children collect recipes from their relatives to go in the cookbooks. Near the end of the summer, assemble these with illustrations on 8-1/2 × 11-inch sheets of paper hole punched and tied with ribbon. Name them "The _____ Family Cookbook." Parents and grandparents will want to help collect recipes, but let the children write, design, and assemble them.

Activity: Get a local geneologist to present a program on tracing your family's roots. Use the Family Tree form to trace family backgrounds with the help of a grandparent.

THEME: FRIENDS

Sometimes old friends go to camp together, and camp is definitely the place to make new friends! Start off this program with a discussion of being, making, and having friends at camp.

Bulletin Board Idea: Friendship faces. Paper plates, yarn, markers, glue, mirror. Each child gets a paper plate. Have them take turns looking at themselves in the mirror and drawing their own faces on a paper plate. Have them glue yarn hair and draw eyes that match their own in color. Attach these to a wall with the label "Camp Wanna-Read's Friendship Faces."

PROGRAM 1

Age: Ps—Grade 2

Books

- Browne, Anthony. *Willy and Hugh.* Knopf, 1991.
- Coleridge, Ann. *The Friends of Emily Culpepper.* Putnam, 1987.
- Henkes, Kevin. *Chester's Way.* Greenwillow, 1988.

Family Tree

YOUR NAME

Brothers and Sisters

NAME
BORN WHERE: WHEN:
NAME
BORN WHERE: WHEN:
NAME
BORN WHERE: WHEN:
NAME
BORN WHERE: WHEN:

Mother's Brothers and Sisters

NAME
MARRIED TO:
CHILDREN:
NAME
MARRIED TO:
CHILDREN:
NAME
MARRIED TO:
CHILDREN:
NAME
MARRIED TO:
CHILDREN:

MOTHER
BORN:
WHERE:
DIED:
WHERE:

GRANDFATHER
BORN:
WHERE:
DIED:
WHERE:

GRANDMOTHER
BORN:
WHERE:
DIED:
WHERE:

GREAT GRANDFATHER
BORN:
WHERE:
DIED:
WHERE:

GREAT GRANDMOTHER
BORN:
WHERE:
DIED:
WHERE:

GREAT GRANDFATHER
BORN:
WHERE:
DIED:
WHERE:

GREAT GRANDMOTHER
BORN:
WHERE:
DIED:
WHERE:

FATHER
BORN:
WHERE:
DIED:
WHERE:

GRANDFATHER
BORN:
WHERE:
DIED:
WHERE:

GRANDMOTHER
BORN:
WHERE:
DIED:
WHERE:

GREAT GRANDFATHER
BORN:
WHERE:
DIED:
WHERE:

GREAT GRANDMOTHER
BORN:
WHERE:
DIED:
WHERE:

GREAT GRANDFATHER
BORN:
WHERE:
DIED:
WHERE:

GREAT GRANDMOTHER
BORN:
WHERE:
DIED:
WHERE:

Spouse

NAME
BORN WHERE: WHEN:
DIED WHERE: WHEN:

Your Children

NAME
BORN WHERE: WHEN:
NAME
BORN WHERE: WHEN:
NAME
BORN WHERE: WHEN:
NAME
BORN WHERE: WHEN:

Father's Brothers and Sisters

NAME
MARRIED TO:
CHILDREN:
NAME
MARRIED TO:
CHILDREN:
NAME
MARRIED TO:
CHILDREN:
NAME

- King, Larry. *Because of Lozo Brown.* Viking Kestrel, 1988.
- Priceman, Marjorie. *Friend or Frog.* Houghton Mifflin, 1989.

Films

- *Frog and Toad Are Friends.* Churchill, 1985, 18 min.
- *Mole as Watchmaker.* Phoenix, 1976, 6 min.
- *The New Friend.* Made to Order Library Productions, 1981, 11 min.

Fingerplay

One hand can wave (wave)
One hand can snap (snap)
But it needs a friend if it wants to clap. (clap)

Action Rhyme

The more we get together, the happier we'll be
The more we get together, the happier we'll be
'Cause your friends are my friends and my friends are your friends. . .
And if we get together, we have a big party! (pronounced Par-teeee)

Children stand in a large circle and take steps inward while saying the first two lines. All children point to each other on the third line. All run to the center and throw their arms up on last line. Share the poem *Together* from the picture book of the same name by Ella Lyon George, Orchard, 1989.

Activity: With the book *The Friends of Emily Culpepper,* bring a jar and ask the children if they would put their tiny friends in a jar. For fun, each draw a small person and put it in the jar! The children will all want to see it and hear the story.

Activity: Mirror a friend (for ages 5 and up). Two children sit facing each other. One child of the two must mirror the actions of the other. The other child tries to make the mirror child "mess up." Have the two children sit in the middle of the circle and change players frequently.

PATTERN 8

Frog Clicker

Craft: Hands in Friendship. You need styrofoam meat trays, construction paper, tempera paint (two contrasting colors). Pour one color into each tray. Friends in the group make their handprints together on the paper. Provide enough so evey child gets a picture. Give each child a colored dot. Children that have the same color make their handprints together so no one is left out.

Activity: Frog clickers. Read Marjorie Priceman's book *Friend or Frog.* Then gather: glue, scissors, markers, brown, green, and white construction paper, and one baby food jar lid. Cut out the patterns from construction paper. The green paper is for the frog, the brown for the lilly pad, and the white for the lilly. Draw the front of the water lilly on the pattern piece. Glue the lilly pad on the top of the jar lid, the frog on to the lilly pad, and the lilly on to the lilly pad. Draw some eyes on the frog. After the glue dries, press in the center of the jar lid, making a clicking frog noise. See Pattern 8.

Activity: Storytime tree. Have children bring in photographs of themselves or take polaroid pictures. Make a tree shape on a bulletin board and use the photographs as leaves.

PROGRAM 2

Age: Grades 3 and up

Books

- Adler, C.S. *Always and Forever Friends.* Ticknor & Fields, 1988.
- DeClements, Barthe. *Five Finger Discount.* Delacorte, 1989.
- Leverich, Kathleen. *Best Enemies.* Greenwillow, 1989.
- Livingston, Myra Cohn. *I Like You If You Like Me.* Margaret K. McElderry, 1987.
- Pevsner, Stella. *The Night the Whole Class Slept Over.* Clarion, 1991.

Activity: Friendship stick. You need: Sticks, dowels, or paper towel tubes, yarn in various colors, glue, various small items such as feathers, beads, small toys, etc. Children glue down one end of a piece of yarn, and then begin wrapping it around their stick. As the yarn nears its end, kids glue it with a few inches left hanging down. Tie the feathers, trinkets, or beads on as "charms." Charms can also be made from cardboard and felt scraps. Make a mini portrait of your friend to put on the stick! These friendship sticks can be exchanged or hung on the wall.

Poetry: Read some poems aloud from the book *I Like You If You Like Me* by Livingston. Put together your own book entitled "Friendship is. . ." with poems, drawings, and stories contributed by the children.

Special Project: Does your town have a sister city? If it does, find out about it—how it was chosen, what kinds of people live there, what their children do. Find a suitable group of children for your library kids to write to in the sister city, such as a church or library group. Send them individual letters or a group letter with illustrations and wait for their response. If your town does not have a sister city, see if your library group can informally adopt a city or group.

THEME: YOU!

Who goes to Camp Wanna-Read? You do!

Age: Grades 3 and up

Books

- Ashabranner, Brent. *People Who Make A Difference.* Cobble Hill, 1989.
- Auch, Mary Jane. *Mom is Dating Weird Wayne.* Holiday House, 1988.
- Little, Jean. *Hey World, Here I Am!* Harper & Row, 1986.
- McKenna, Colleen Shaunessy. *Too Many Murphys.* Scholastic, 1988.

- Park, Barbara. *Rosie Swanson, Fourth Grade Geek for President*. Knopf, 1991.

Films

- *Ramona's Bad Day*. Churchill, 1988, 27 min.
- *The Runt*. CRM McGraw Hill, 1976, 13 min.

Poetry: Read aloud the poem "Hey World, Here I Am" from the book of the same title.

Activity: Autograph books. You need cardboard and wallpaper for covers, paper for the interior pages, yarn, staples, or rings for binding. Assemble the books and brainstorm titles for them such as Friendship Folder or Book Buddies. Have an autograph party! This is a great way to start off the summer with a group and break the ice. Have a contest to see who can get or give the most autographs in two minutes. Or, give prizes for the funniest, silliest, etc, autograph signed. You might also read out the names of famous book characters and have everyone sign their autographs exactly as they think a character might, such as Ramona Quimby or one of Mr. Popper's Penguins.

THEME: SCARY STORIES

A tradition at camp is the scary campfire tale. Turn off all the lights and use only a flashlight to light your face as you tell the story. Play a little scary background music or sound effects. Be sure there are no children under the age of seven.

Age: Grades 3 and up

Books

- Cecil, Laura, ed. *Boo! Stories to Make You Jump*. Greenwillow, 1991.
- Cole, Joanna, ed. *The Scary Book*. Morrow, 1991.
- MacDonald, Margaret Read. *When the Lights Go Out: Twenty Scary Stories to Tell*. H.W. Wilson, 1988.

- San Souci, Robert. *Short and Shivery: Thirty Chilling Tales*. Doubleday, 1987.
- Yolen, Jane. *Things That Go Bump In the Night*. Harper & Row, 1989.

Film

- *The Ghost of Thomas Kempe*. MTI Teleprograms, 1979, 48 min.

Activity: Who's Got the Ghost. Make a ghost by wrapping a kleenex around another kleenex and closing with a rubber band to form the head. Sit in a large circle with your hands clasped in back. The person who is "It" stands in the middle with eyes closed. Play some scary music. When the music is turned on, the ghost is passed from child to child. When the music goes off, whoever is "It" must guess who has the ghost. "It" gets three guesses, and if a guess is correct, then the person with the ghost is now "It."

Epitaphs: Epitaphs are short poems of about four lines that are meant to be chiseled in stone—in a cemetary! Have the children write epitaphs about book characters. Epitaphs rhyme with no set pattern. Epitaphs also begin with "Here Lies. . . ." Some epitaphs have a humorous twist to them:

> Here lies Jason Maces
> Who played his poker sharp
> 'Til one day he played five aces
> Now he plays a harp.

> Under this stone lies Horace Blue
> Who had a pistol, thirty-two.
> To see if it was dirty, into it he blew,
> The gun went off, and he did too.

Invent a Ghost: Do some research about local haunted buildings and tell these stories of alleged ghosts to the children. Remind them of the ghost in the New York Public Library in the movie *Ghostbusters*. As a group, write a story about the haunting of your library complete with characters from the group of children and illustrations.

THEME: GAMES

Games and sports abound at camp. Sometimes there are special sports and game camps.

Age: Grades 3 and up

Books

- Raskin, Ellen. *The Westing Game.* Dutton, 1978.
- Sleator, William. *Interstellar Pig.* Dutton, 1984.
- Slote, Alfred. *The Trading Game.* J.B. Lippincott, 1990.
- Van Allsburg, Chris. *Jumanji.* Houghton Mifflin, 1981.

Film: *The Amazing Bone.* Weston Woods, 1985, 11 min.

Activity: Silly Stories. Everyone sits in a circle for this game. The object of the game is to tell a true story that sounds like a lie or a lie that sounds like a true story. Players take turns relating true or imaginary information about themselves. The librarian should set the tone with something like "I have a pet snake, but my mother is allergic to his scales." After each turn the group must judge—fact or fiction? The round is won by the person if the group thinks it is fiction but it is actually fact or vice versa. Hand out bookmarks or silly prizes (such as plastic glasses with moustaches) for the most outrageous or strange story. Remind the kids that sometimes truth is stranger than fiction, so it is not always necessary to tell a lie!

Activity: String game. You need a ball of string and scissors. Cut 75 or 100 strings of various lengths and hide them around the room before the children arrive. Divide the children into two teams and tell them you have hidden the string and they must find it. The object of the game is to tie the pieces of string together. The team with the longest string at the end of the game wins. Since the strings are different lengths, the team that gets the most strings will not necessarily be the winner. When it seems the strings have all been found, stretch them out next to each other to compare.

Activity: Jokes. Along with your games program, try holding a joke-telling hour. Have the children come in with their best jokes, rhymes, limericks, riddles, or tongue twisters. Try to videotape this for local cable. Hand out ribbons for best joke, worst joke, longest joke, etc. Limericks can be found in *With a Deep Sea Smile*, Virginia Tashjian, Little Brown, 1974. Some books with tongue twisters are:

- Gackenbach, Dick. *Timid Timothy's Tongue Twisters.* Holiday House, 1986.
- Obligado, Lillian. *Faint Frogs Feeling Feverish.* Viking, 1983.
- Scwartz, Alvin. *A Twister of Twists, A Tangler of Tongues.* Lippincott, 1972.
- ———. *Busy Buzzing Bumblebees and Other Tongue Twisters.* Harper and Row, 1982.
- Seuss, Dr. *Oh, Say Can You Say!* Beginner Books, 1979.

Activity: Design a board game. Suggest the children get partners and make up their own board game. They can design a board and make up questions that go on cards. Dice, a spinner, or colored dots on the cards indicate the number of spaces a player moves. After viewing the film *The Amazing Bone,* you could design an Amazing Bone Game.

THEME: KITES

What better place for a kite flying contest than camp? Display lots of colorful kites in your children's area. Tell some kite stories and then do some of the following activities.

Age: All Ages

Books

- Brock, Ray. *Go Fly a Kite.* Bookstore Press, 1976.
- Demi. *Kites and Dragonflies.* Harcourt, Brace, Jovanovich, 1986.
- Gray, Genevieve. *A Kite for Benny.* McGraw Hill, 1972.
- Reeser, Michael. *Huan Ching and the Golden Kite.* Raintree, 1989.
- Yolen, Jane. *The Emperor and the Kite.* Philomel, 1988.

Film: *How to Be a Perfect Person in Just Three Days.* Learning Corporation of America, 1985, 55 min.

Activity: Have the children write a shape poem or story in the shape of a kite. Use topics like "Where my kite goes when the string breaks" or "Where I would fly if I were a kite." For the younger children, record their responses to these ideas on a large poster and mount on the shape of a kite. Display in the children's area. Some useful kite patterns are found in *Paperworks* by Virginie Fowler (Prentice Hall, 1982) and *Bags Are Big: A Paper Bag Craft Book.* by Nancy Renfro (Nancy Renfro Studios, 1987). Some poems to get them started are: "Kite", Anonymous, *Read Aloud Rhymes for the Very Young,* p. 33, Jack Prelutsky, Knopf, 1986; or "To a Red Kite" by Lillian Moore, *Sing a Song of Popcorn,* p. 33, Bernice Schenk deRegniers, Scholastic, 1988.

RELATED ACTIVITIES

Plan some brown bag book seminars for your library. Plan about 30 minutes of stories during lunch. Set up tables in your program room, or do this outside if you have a shady area. Everyone brings their own bag lunch to eat. Children are accompanied by at least one parent, but the whole family should be invited. As the participants eat their own lunches, tell stories, publicize events at the library, or read aloud a chapter from a book. If you read a chapter, people will want to come back every week until you are finished. Choose a classic or modern standard that is about ten chapters long and appeals to all ages. Jim Trelease's *The New Read Aloud Handbook* (Jim Trelease, Penguin, 1989) is a good source for finding stories to read aloud. Do this activity once a week for eight to ten weeks. It makes a nice change of pace from going to a fast food restaurant for lunch. Ask for volunteers to take turns reading or telling stories. Purchase some brown lunch sacks and glue a bibliography of the stories you use or or other information to the sacks. Put take-home coloring sheets and library publicity items in the sacks and pass them out as people leave. This activity takes little planning but will get you many thanks from harassed parents.

You could also make these more formal events, with storytelling going on for the children and mini workshops going on for the adults. Use topics that can be addressed in a short period of time, such as "Ten reasons to read aloud to your child." (See "Tips for Parents" in chapter 5)

COMMUNITY PARTNERSHIPS

Campfire or local camp counselors can present programs for you. Ask Campfire to come and do a program on camping out or invite a counselor to talk about going to camp. Consult your phone directory for the phone number of your local campfire council. Contact the following organizations for information on camp.

American Camping Association.
Bradford Woods
5000 State Road North
Martinsville, IN 46151-7902
(317) 342-8456

This organization accredits camps and certifies camp directors.

C.A.M.P. (Camping Association for Mutual Progress)
(Contact either Camp Longhorn or Camp Stewart)

This organization conducts educational programs, publishes camping magazines, publishes *Camping Magazine Parents Guide to Accredited Camps,* holds an annual CAMPference in Austin. Free newsletter.

Camp Longhorn
PO Box 60
Burnet, Texas 78611
(512) 756-4560

Camp Stewart
Hunt, Texas 78024
(512) 238-4670

Hold a mini CAMPference in your library at the beginning of the summer. Gather together as much information as possible on local camps. Gather books on camping also, invite a guest speaker and the public. you could also publicize your reading club and summer programs at this event. Or, do this as part of another program.

MORE CAMP BOOKS

Ps—Grade 2

Armitage, Rhonda & David. *One Moonlit Night*. Dutton, 1983.

Brown, Myra. *Pip Camps Out*. Golden Gate, 1966.

Carrick, Carol. *Sleep Out*. Houghton Mifflin, 1979.

Henkes, Kevin. *Bailey Goes Camping*. Greenwillow, 1985.

Locker, Thomas. *Where the River Begins*. Dial, 1984.

Maestro, Giulio. *Camping Out*. Crown, 1985.

Marshall, James. *The Cut-Ups at Camp Custer*. Viking, 1990.

Mayer, Mercer. *Just Me and My Dad*. Golden, 1977.

Maynard, Joyce. *Camp-Out*. HBJ, 1985.

Parrish, Peggy. *Amelia Bedelia Goes Camping*. Greenwillow, 1985.

Robbins, Joan. *Addie Runs Away*. Harper & Row, 1989.

Rockwell, Anne. *The Night We Slept Outside*. Macmillan, 1983.

Schulman, Janet. *Camp Kee-Wees Secret Weapon*. Greenwillow, 1979.

Shulevitz, Uri. *Dawn*. Farrar, Straus & Giroux, 1974.

Thomson, Vivian. *Camp-in-the-Yard*. Holiday House, 1961.

Warren, Cathy. *Ten Alarm Camp Out*. Lothrop, Lee & Shepherd, 1983.

Weiss, Niki. *Battle Day at Camp Belmont*. Greenwillow, 1985.

Williams, Vera. *Three Days on a River in a Red Canoe*. Greenwillow, 1981.

Yolen, Jane. *The Giants Go Camping*. Seabury, 1979.

Grade 3 and up

Angell, Judy. *It's Summertime, It's Tuffy*. Dell, 1979.

Christian, Mary Blount. *Mystery at Camp Triumph*. Albert Whitman, 1986.

Coville, Bruce. *Some of My Best Friends Are Monsters*. Simon & Schuster, 1988.

Delton, Judy. *The Mystery of the Haunted Cabin*. Houghton Mifflin, 1986.

Duncan, Audry D. *Camp Manchester Eighty-Three*. Carlton, 1989

Gauch, Patricia Lee. *Night Talks*. Putnam, 1983.

Gitenstein, Judy. *Summer Camp*. Bantam, 1984.

Holl, Kristy. *The Haunting of Cabin Thirteen*. Atheneum, 1987.

Landon, Lucinda. *Meg MacIntosh and the Mystery at Camp Creepy*. Little Brown, 1990.

Lane, Carolyn. *Ghost Island*. Houghton Mifflin, 1985.

Levinson, Nancy. *Your Friend, Natalie Popper*. Lodestar Dutton, 1990.

Levy, Elizabeth. *Dracula is a Pain in the Neck*. Harper & Row, 1983.

McKenna, Colleen O'Shaughnessey. *Eenie, Meanie, Murphy, No*. Scholastic, 1982.

Martin, Anne. *Bummer Summer*. Holiday House, 1983.

Norby, Lisa. *Crazy Campout*. Knopf, 1989.

O'Connor, Jim & Jane. *The Ghost in Tent Nineteen*. Random House, 1988.

Park, Barbara. *Buddies*. Knopf, 1985.

Pravda, Myra & Weiland. *Off to Camp*. JSP Publications, 1989.

Schneider, Susan. *Please Send Junk Food*. Putnam, 1985.

Stolz, Mary. *Wonderful, Terrible Time*. Harper & Row, 1967.

A PUPPET SHOW SCRIPT

Compare different versions of *Little Red Riding Hood* before presenting this Camp Wanna-Read puppet show.

Ages: All Ages

Books

- Galdone, Paul. *Little Red Riding Hood.* McGraw Hill 1974.
- Hogrogian, Nonny. *The Renowned History of Little Red Riding Hood.* Crowell, 1967.
- Hyman, Tina Schart. *Little Red Riding Hood.* Holiday House, 1983.
- Marshall, James. *Red Riding Hood.* Dial, 1987.

Film: *Red Riding Hood.* Weston Woods, 1991, 8 min.

LITTLE RED GOES TO CAMP

A Puppet Play in one act

Characters:

Little Red
Wolf in Camp Counselors Clothing
Granny

Props:

- Tent drawn on posterboard with dowel attached.
- Small backpack with a hole in the bottom so Granny can come out of it.
- Cardboard book or a real one attached to dowel
- Sign that says "Camp Wanna-Read" attached to stage.

Music up, then fade out. Little Red is skipping along singing the camp song "A-camping we will go". She notices audience.

Little Red: Oh, hello! My Name is Little Red and I'm on my way to Camp Wanna-Read. I just love to go to camp. We do all sorts of fun things like swimming and playing and drawing and reading. But the reason I like camp the most is because my Grandmother is the camp counselor!

Little Red continues to walk on and looks at sign that says Camp Wanna-Read.

Little Red: Here's camp. I wonder where my Granny is? Yo-hoo, oh Grandmother, here I am, your favorite granddaughter!

Wolf: *(Start out in wolf voice then change to falsetto)* Here I am. . .Ahem. . .I mean here I am Little Red! I've been waiting for you to get here so I could eat LUNCH!

Little Red: But Granny! You Know I always wait for the other campers to arrive before I eat.

Wolf: Oh, silly Red! You don't have to eat, only I do!

Little Red: Granny, where are the other campers? I don't see anyone.

Wolf: Of course you don't my dear. They are all . . .uh. . . playing hide and seek! I can't see them anywhere either.

Little Red: You should be able to see them, Granny, with those great big eyes you have.

Wolf: Ah. . .Yes, but my eyesight is getting dim. . . *(Noises from offstage of Granny struggling in backpack)*

Little Red: Granny, what's that noise?

Wolf: Those are, uhh, nature sounds dear, can't you tell? It's just the birds singing, the frogs croaking. Now come along, lets EAT!

Little Red: I'm sure I can't hear them as well as you can with those great big ears of yours. But Granny, surely you remember that we always race around the camp on the first day. You have to give me a chance to beat you! Now come on, READY SET GO!

Little Red and wolf run back and forth across stage. Wolf starts to puff noisily and then falls down exhausted.

Little Red: Why Granny, this is the first year I've ever beaten you! Granny, you sure are breathing hard. Are you O.K.? You ought to be able to breathe with that great big nose of yours!!

Wolf: Oh. . .uhhh. . .yes, well I'm out of shape. *(Wolf continues to breathe hard)* Can we eat NOW!?!

Little Red: But Granny, you know we have to put up my tent before we eat lunch. Now come on, get up and help me.

Wolf: Oh, all right.

Wolf stuggles with tent and Little Red makes comments such as "A little to the left, hurry up now," etc. Finally after a few seconds of struggle, tent falls on Wolf. Wolf howls with pain.

Little Red: Why Granny, you sure can yell with that great big mouth of yours.

Wolf: But I'd rather eat with it! I'm going to have my lunch NOW!! *(Wolf begins to lunge at Little Red, but Red suddenly picks up a book and Wolf is blocked by it.)*

Little Red: Oh Granny! Look, it's our favorite story "The Wolf and the Seven Little Kids!" *(or some other Wolf story)*

Wolf: What!?! A story about a Wolf? Read it to me, PLeeeeaase! *(In a whiny voice)*

Little Red: Now Granny, you know you like to read this story aloud to me. Come on read! *(Gives book to Wolf)*

Wolf: But, but. . . . *(Wolf starts to cry)* I can't read.

Little Red: What do you mean you can't read. Wait a minute! Your not my Granny! You're the BIG BAD WOLF! What have you done with my Granny, you mean ol' nasty wolf?? *(Little Red grabs book and wolf continues to cry)*

Wolf: Oh, your Granny's all right. Please read me the story about the Wolf. I've never heard a story about a wolf before.

Little Red: I don't know. . .well, OK. I know! I'll read you this story if you promise to give me my Granny and never be mean again.

Wolf: I will! I will! I promise! *(Wolf runs and gets backpack and lets granny out from where she has been the whole time. Granny makes comments like "whew, I was beginning to wonder if I was ever going to get out of there")*

Granny: Come along now Wolf and Little Red, it's time for that story. *(To Little Red)* Maybe if we teach that Wolf to read he will learn to cook some other dishes besides Grannies and little girls in red hoods! *(All 3 exit with Granny reading* "Once upon a time" *etc.)*

Music up.

Note: this puppet play can be extended by adding other events that happen at camp such as arts and crafts (wolf gets glued to a tree) or swimming (Little Red has to rescue Wolf). Please adapt it as necessary for your situation.

2 GET WILD!

Stalk the wild side. Get Wild with the outdoors, nature, animals, plants, and fossils! Preface this week with a poster or bulletin board showing all the things that happen and the animals you meet outdoors.

THEME: SOMETHING FISHY!

Go fishing at the library!

Age: Ps—Grade 2

Books

- Afanasyev, Alexander. *The Fool and the Fish: A Tale from Russia*. Dial, 1990.
- Ehlert, Lois. *Fish Eyes: A Book You Can Count On*. HBJ, 1990.
- Sadler, Marilyn. *Alaistair Underwater*. Simon and Schuster, 1990.
- Yorinks, Arthur. *Louis the Fish*. Farrar, 1980.

Films

- *Fish is Fish*. Distribution 16, 1985, 5 min.
- *Swimmy*. Conn Films, Incorporated, 1969, 6 min.
- *The Fisherman and His Wife*. Weston Woods, 1970, 20 min.

Opening: Decorate your storytime area with blue streamers and paper fish to simulate an underwater atmosphere. Serve

PATTERN 9

Flannel Board Fish

FIGURE 2-1

Paper Plate Fish

fish-shaped crackers. Set up a small, simple aquarium and let the children observe the fish in their natural habitat. (A small goldfish bowl, gravel, and a goldfish can be purchased at a pet store for about $20.)

Fingerplay: (Use Pattern 9 to make a flannel board for this fingerplay.)

Five little fish swam by the shore,
One ate a worm and then there were four.
Four little fish swam in the sea,
One blew a bubble, and then there were three.
Three little fish swam in the blue,
One swam in seaweed and then there were two.
Two little fish swam in the sun,
One talked to clam, and then there was one.
One little fish, splash, splash, splash,
His mother called and he went home in a flash!

Activity: Bring a dish tub full of water and demonstrate different objects that will float in water, such as Ivory soap or corks. Put a blue ribbon on the wall for a water line. Tell the kids they are now underwater. Ask them to draw the fish they would most like to be on large pieces of paper, then color then color and cut out. Hang them on the wall, and now you have an "aquarium" on the wall.

Put a clear glass bowl of water on top of an overhead projector and drop various colors of food coloring into it. With the water shimmering on the wall, you will feel that you are really underwater. This is also a good lesson in color combinations.

Have the children pretend they can breathe underwater. Pantomime what it would be like to do every day activities underwater, such as brushing your teeth. Would the tooth-paste float away? Have the children illustrate what it would be like to live underwater—what would we use for transportation? What would we eat?

Craft: Paper plate fish. Give each child a paper plate with a triangular mouth shape cut out. Let them glue the triangle opposite the mouth to serve as a tail. Have them decorate to

PATTERN 10

Hanging Fish

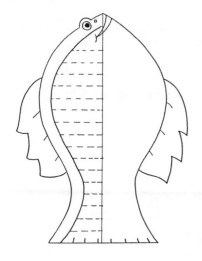

look like their favorite storybook fish. Glue on to blue butcher paper to make a group mural.

Craft: Hanging Fish. Make copies of Pattern 10 from the appendix and fold in half lengthwise. Now cut out the fish. Cut on the dotted lines to the inside curve of the fish. Unfold and bend every other strip backward. Decorate both sides of the fish and hang as mobiles.

THEME: ANIMAL TRACKS

Track the wild beasts!

Age: Grades 2 and up

Books

- Arnosky, Jim. *Crinkleroot's Guide to Walking in Wild Places*. Bradbury, 1990.
- Arnosky, Jim. *Crinkleroot's Guide to Animal Tracks and Wildlife Signs*. Putnam, 1979.
- Baylor, Byrd. *We Walk in Sandy Places*. Scribner's, 1976.
- Murie, Johan Olaus. *Field Guide to Animal Tracks*. Houghton Mifflin, 1975.
- Pearce, Querida. *Nature's Footprints in the Forest*. Silver Press, 1990.

Activity: Animal Tracks. Animals can sometimes be found close to the city. Take the children to a sandy spot and practice tracking. Have them walk, run, and jump, then measure the different strides from heel to toe. Have them turn around while you make some tracks. See if they can imitate your movements just by the tracks you have left. Look for animal tracks now. This activity can also be done indoors; two children draw around each other's feet while walking on butcher paper. Measure the distance between the two and compare stride lengths.

THEME: FOSSIL FINDS

A sure fire favorite, discover dinosaurs and fossils.

PROGRAM 1

Age: Ps—Grade 2

Books

- Blackwood, May. *Derek, the Knitting Dinosaur*. Carolrhoda, 1990.
- Donnelly, Liza. *Dinosaur Garden*. Scholastic, 1989.
- Hopkins, Lee Bennett. *Dinosaurs*. HBJ, 1987.
- Moseley, Francis. *The Dinosaur Eggs*. Francis Barrons, 1988.
- Taylor, Scott. *Dinosaur James*. Morrow Junior Books, 1990.

Film: *Danny and the Dinosaur*. Weston Woods, 1990, 9 min.

Share the poem "Fossils" by Lillian Moore from *Dinosaurs* by Myra Cohn Livingston.
Use the following song to the tune of "The Wheels on the Bus"

The Tyrannosaurus Rex went "ROAR, ROAR, ROAR"
"ROAR, ROAR, ROAR; ROAR ROAR ROAR"
The Tyrannosaurus Rex went "ROAR, ROAR, ROAR"
All around the swamp.

Also:

PATTERN 11

Dinosaur Egg

The Pterodactyl's wing went flap flap flap.
The Stegosaurus' tail went poke poke poke.
The Brontosaurus' feet went stomp stomp stomp.

Activity: Have a fossil hunt. Fill a box with sand and lots of toy plastic dinosaurs. Let the children take turns hunting for fossils. Make sure you have enough for everyone. These plastic dinosaurs can be purchased in bags of 20 for a few dollars. Using playdough or playclay, let the children can make fossils by pressing the plastic dinosaurs into the clay. Let the imprints dry.

Activity: Dinosaur parade. Each child pretends to be a different dinosaur and marches like that beast to music. Some good music to use is Hap Palmer's album *Pretend, Once Upon a Dinosaur* by Jane Murphy, or "Dinosaurs" from *Monsters and Monstrous Things* by Kimbo Educational.

Craft: Make a dinosaur egg using Pattern 11 from the appendix. Each child draws their own dinosaur to go in the egg. Sing the song "If I had a Dinosaur" from *The Raffi Singable Songbook,* pages 44-45, Crown, 1987.

PATTERN 12

Popcorn Dinosaur

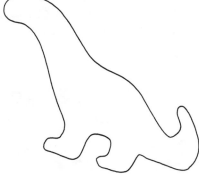

Craft: Popcorn dinosaurs. Give each child a copy of Pattern 12 from the appendix cut from construction paper. Let them glue popcorn all over their dinosaur. They like to eat as much as they glue!

PROGRAM 2

Age: Grades 3 and up

Books

- Arnold, Caroline. *Dinosaur Mountain: Graveyards of the Past.* Clarion, 1990.
- Booth, Jerry. *The Beast Book.* Little Brown, 1988.
- Steiner, Barbara. *Oliver Dibbs and the Dinosaur Cause.* Four Winds, 1986.

Film: *Dinosaur.* Pyramid Films and Video, 1980, 14 min.

Activities

An excellent resource full of exciting ideas on this topic is *The Beast Book* by Jerry Booth. Use any of the following to assure an interesting time:

Geology You Can Eat (pages 20-23). A recipe for a jello desert that looks like rocks but tastes good.

Pigeon-Toed or Dino-Toed? (page 40). Casting footprints in plaster.

Rubber Bones (page 48). Recipe to make bones bounce!

Carbon Copies (page 55). Delicate carbon "fossils" of leaves.

Crazy Crests (pages 87-89). How to make a hadrosaur crest to wear.

The Steggy Story (pages 105-108). How to start and finish your own kids' state fossil campaign. Use the book *Oliver Dibbs and the Dinosaur Cause* with this activity.

THEME: GREEN AND GROWING

Watch out for poison ivy!

Bulletin Board Idea: Make a flowers growing bulletin board: Each child draws a self portrait as a flower (like Pookins in the book *Pookins Gets Her Way*) Put each child's name on the leaves and post on the bulletin board.

PROGRAM 1

Age: Ps—Grade 2

Books

- Ehlert, Lois. *Red Leaf, Yellow Leaf.* HBJ, 1990.
- Fleischman, Sid. *The Scarebird.* Greenwillow, 1988.

- Jenkin-Pearce, Suse. *The Enchanted Garden.* Oxford University Press, 1989.
- Kemp, Anthea. *Mr. Percy's Magic Greenhouse.* Victor Gollancz, 1986.
- Lester, Helen. *Pookins Gets Her Way.* Houghton Mifflin, 1987.

Film: *Watch Out for My Plant.* Barr Films, 1972, 14 min.

Flower Walk: Take the children for a walk and see as many different kinds of flowers as you can. Or bring some different kinds to the storytime area for them to see. Talk about different kinds of vegetables, gardens, plants, etc. Contact a local greenhouse or florist to see if they will come and show their plants or donate flowers for storytime.

Fingerplay:

I rake my garden nice and flat (Rake fingers on flat palm)
Then plant some seeds just like that. ("sprinkle" seeds)
Next comes rain, (rain down fingers like Itsy Bitsy Spider)
And sunshine's glow, (circle arms overhead)
Will make my garden grow and grow! (sprout fingers up like plants growing)

PATTERN 13

Popsickle Stick Scarecrow

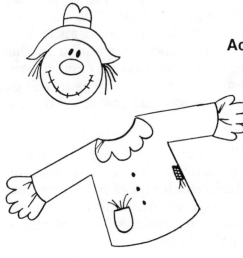

Activities:

Sing "In My Garden" from *The Second Raffi Songbook,* pages 79-80, Crown, 1987.

Talk about gardening and scarecrows. A good book for this is *The Scarebird* by Fleischman. What is the scarecrow's job?

Share poetry from the book *Anna's Garden Songs* by Mary Q. Steele, Greenwillow, 1989.

Tell story and do an activity from *Hidden Stories in Plants* by Anne Pellowski, MacMillan, 1990.

Craft: Popsickle stick scarecrow. Each child needs two popsickle sticks and glue. Cross the sticks and glue together. Decorate with clothing and a head cut from Pattern 13 or make your own.

Action rhyme

I'm a scarecrow, hung on a stick. (Act limp)
When a bird comes, I say "Shoo, bird, quick!" (Flap arms)
When a rabbit comes, I say "Go, run away!" (Wiggle fingers like rabbit ears)
When a farmer comes, I say "Have a nice day!" (Tip hat)

PROGRAM 2

Age: Grade 3 and up

Books

- Alcock, Vivan. *The Monster Garden*. Delacorte, 1988.
- Bjork, Christina. *Linnea's Almanac*. R & S Books, 1989.
- Pellowski, Anne. *Hidden Stories in Plants*. Macmillan, 1990.
- Van Allsburg, Chris. *The Garden of Abdul Gasazi*. Houghton Mifflin, 1979.

Film: *Philly Philodendron*. Films Incorporated, 1973, 12 min.

Activity: Let's pretend. Go outside and do some garden skits and charades. Divide children into groups of no more than seven. Each group creates its own skit and performs it. Write down various themes for skits on paper slips and draw them from a hat. Use such themes as "raccoon eating magical corn," "planting seeds on Mars," or "prehistoric worms in the garden." Have the children make props and costumes from objects found out of doors.

Craft: Vegetable Prints. When cut in half, vegetables make different patterns and shapes to print. Cut various vegetables and fruits and dip the flat surface in tempera paint. Try not to move the vegetable as you press it down and lift it from paper. Experiment with various colors and designs. Note: Styrofoam meat trays make excellent paint holders.

Craft: Carrot necklace. You need carrots, heavy thread, a darning needle and a knife. Wash the carrots and slice them about 1/4-inch thick. Thread your needle with a piece of thread long enough to go over your head and then some. Slip the carrot slices onto the thread by pushing the needle into the center of each slice. Once you have strung enough carrots to fill the thread, lay it on a piece of paper in a dark place to dry with spacing between each carrot slice. it takes about a week for the carrots to dry, but you end up with crinkly orange beads.

THEME: BUG SAFARI

Creepy crawlies and buggy bugs!

Age: Ps—Grade 2

Books

- Carle, Eric. *The Grouchy Ladybug.* Crowell, 1977.
- ———. *The Very Busy Spider.* Philomel, 1986.
- ———. *The Very Quiet Cricket.* Philomel, 1990.
- Kimmell, Eric. *Anansi and the Moss Covered Rock.* Holiday House, 1988.
- Van Allsburg, Chris. *Two Bad Ants.* Houghton Mifflin, 1988.

Fingerplay

I'm a spider (make spider with hands)
I spin, spin, spin (move fingers in spinning motion)
I spin big webs (move hands apart to show a big web)
To catch flies in! ("catch" a fly)

Poetry: "Bugs" by Karla Kuskin from Lee Bennett Hopkins *Surprises.*

Films

- *Anansi the Spider.* Texture Films, 1969, 10 min.
- *A Story, A Story.* Weston Woods, 1973, 10 min.

Craft: Grouchy ladybug. Use a 9-inch red circle for the ladybug's body. Decorate with black dots like a ladybug. Cut four slits in the circle as indicated. Tuck down the piece between the slits and staple in place. Use black pipe cleaners as antennae.

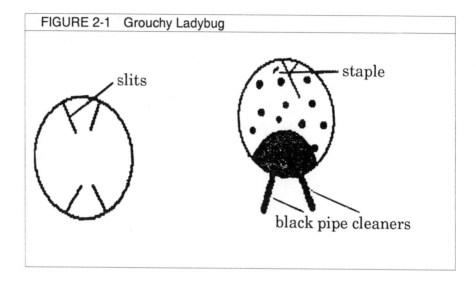

FIGURE 2-1 Grouchy Ladybug

Activity: Anansi Storytime. There are many sources for Anansi stories. A favorite is *Anansi and the Moss Covered Rock.* Check *The Fairy Tale Index* for variations to use.

Craft: Anansi Puppet. Cut out a 6-inch circle from black construction paper and tape it to a popsicle stick. Cut eight 6 × 1-inch strips of black paper and fold them accordian style—as Anansi's legs. Tape them evenly around the circle. Draw Anansi's face. Sing "Anansi" from *The Raffi Singable Songbook,* pages 8-11 (Crown, 1987) using these puppets.

Craft: Spider Webs. Gather up variously colored paper plates, hole punch, tape, 18-inch piece of white yarn. Wrap tape around the end of the yarn to keep it from fraying. Knot the other end. Punch holes around the perimeter of the paper plate. Lace the yarn through the holes to form web-like designs.

THEME: WATER WORKS

Canoeing, sailing, and swimming—water works!

Age: Grades 3 and up.

Books

- Alexander, Ellen. *The Llama and the Great Flood*. Thomas Y. Crowell, 1989.
- Doubilet, Anne. *Under the Sea From A to Z*. Crown, 1991.
- Mahy, Margaret. *The Seven Chinese Brothers*. Scholastic, 1989.
- Saunders, Susan. *The Daring Rescue of Marlon the Swimming Pig*. Random House, 1987.
- Scwartz, David. *The Hidden Life of the Pond*. Crown, 1988.

Film: *Burt Dow, Deep Water Man*. Weston Woods, 1973, 10 min.

Start out by sharing the story *The Seven Chinese Brothers* by Mahy. Ask the children what they would do if they could, like the first Chinese Brother, hold back the sea. Share a chapter from the Saunders Book and tell *The Llama and the Great Flood*.

Activity: Waves in a Bottle. Using a clear glass container, turpentine, and rubbing alcohol, pour equal amounts of the alcohol and turpentine into the bottle until it is full. Add a few drops of food coloring. Dry the rim of the bottle completely. Put a little white glue on the inner rim of the cap. Put the cap on the bottle. Wrap the edge of the cap in waterproof tape to keep it from leaking. When the glue has dried, slowly tip the bottle on its side, then stand it up again. The heavier liquid, turpentine, will stay in the bottom part of the bottle. The lighter liquid, the rubbing alcohol, will stay near the top. You will see waves that curl and break where the two liquids meet.

Craft: Sea Salt Paint.

2 Tsp. salt
bowl & spoon
1 Tsp. liquid starch
1 Tsp. Water
Tempera paint
paintbrush
paper

Mix all the ingredients together in the bowl and stir with the spoon, pouring the salt in last. Now paint on a dark colored paper to make an underwater textural scene!

THEME: A HERD OF BIRDS

Birdwatching is a popular pastime.

Age: All Ages

Books

- Anderson, Hans Christian. *The Nightingale*. North South Books, 1989.
- Kent, Jack. *Round Robin*. Prentice Hall, 1982.
- Palacek, Josef and Libuse. *The Magic Grove*. North South Books, 1990.
- Troughton, Joanna. *How the Birds Changed Their Feathers: A South American Indian Folktale*. Harper, 1986.
- VanLaan, Nancy. *Rainbow Crow: A Lenape Tale*. Knopf, 1989.

Films

- *How the Kiwi Lost His Wings*. Churchill, 1981, 12 min.
- *The Happy Owls*. Weston Woods, 1969, 6 min.

Fingerplay

Five baby birds, waiting for spring,
The first baby bird began to sing,
The second baby bird flapped its wings,
The third baby bird said "Tweet, tweet, tweet",
The fourth baby bird said "Let's eat!"
The fifth baby bird said "No, let's play."
But along came a cat and they all flew away.

Craft: Make "Round Robin": Each child needs a 3-inch circle cut from brown paper and a 5-inch circle cut from red paper. Glue these together to form the head (brown) and body (red).

PATTERN 14

Hanging Bird

Add a paper beak and pipe cleaner legs. Draw an eye, and glue feathers on for wings.

OR, use Pattern 14 from the appendix and make birds. Trace the body and two wings onto construction paper. Cut out the body and wings. Fold the wings on the dotted line, apply glue on the folded part and glue one wing to either side of body. Decorate with eyes, beak, and use yarn to hang up.

Special Project: Make feathered friends! Designate a tree close to your library as a bird sanctuary. Make these special feeders. Gather cookie cutters, stale bread, peanut butter, sunflower seeds, and straws. Cut various shapes from the bread using the cookie cutters. Spread peanut butter on each piece and then cover with sunflower seeds. The seeds will stick to the peanut butter. Punch a hole in each shape with a staw. String some yarn through the hole and hang from your sanctuary tree. Keep a written or illustrated record in the library of the birds that visit the tree. Place it where children can read it or add to it if they like.

MUNCHABUNCH

Cooking! What a delicious thing to do in the library! Kids love to eat and they love to make things, so this week focus on books and activities about cooking and eating.

Some poetry to use with this project:

> *The Random House Book of Poetry* compiled by Jack Prelusky, (Random House, 1983): "My Mouth" by Arnold Adoff, "Egg Thoughts" by Russell Hoban, "Oodles of Noodles" by Lucia and James Hymes, "Pie Problem" by Shel Silverstein.

Pack up a picnic basket full of the picture books you will be using. Make it a special event to reach in and pull out the books one by one. You might also want to wear a chef's hat or apron to storytime this week.

THEME: TEA TIME

Tell children of the simple pleasures of a gracious tea time!

Age: Ps—Grade 2

Books

- Galdone, Paul. *The Gingerbread Boy.* Seabury, 1975.
- Kerr, Judith. *The Tiger Who Came to Tea.* Coward McCann, 1969.
- Noble, Trinka Hankes. *The King's Tea.* Dial, 1979.
- Shulevitz, Uri. *One Monday Morning.* Scribner's, 1967.

Films

- *Sea Dream.* Phoenix, 1980, 6 min.

PATTERN 15

Gingerbread Boy's Head

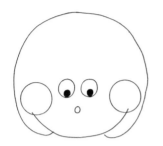

PATTERN 16

Gingerbread Boy's Body

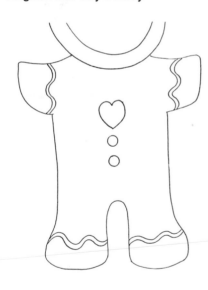

• *One Monday Morning.* Weston Woods, 1972, 10 min.

Poem and Fingerplay

"A Cup of Tea" from *Children's Counting Out Rhymes, Fingerplays, Bounce Ball Chants, And Other Rhythms.* Gloria T. Delamar, Macfarland, 1983.

Here's a cup, and here's a cup, and here's a pot of tea.
Pour a cup, and pour a cup, and come and drink with me.

Or use "Tea Party" from the *Scott Foresman Anthology of Children's Literature* by Harvey Behn, Zena Sutherland, and Myra Cohn Livingston, eds., Scott Foresman, 1984.

Craft: Cookie Cutter Art. You need variously shaped cookie cutters, styrofoam meat trays filled with a little poster paint, and construction paper. Children dip the cookie cutters into the paint and make prints on the construction paper. Let them make invitations to tea for the king in *One Monday Morning* or *The King's Tea.*

Craft: Gingerbread Boy puppet. Use Patterns 15 and 16 for sack puppets with The Gingerbread Boy. Let the children participate in the story by making the puppets say the lines of the Gingerbread Boy.

Activity: Find the Gingerbread boy game. After reading the story, hide a brown paper Gingerbread man in the storytime area. Let the children take turns guessing where you hid him while you give them clues. The child who guesses correctly gets to then pass out gingerbread cookies to all the children.

THEME: PASTA POWER

Spaghetti, spaghetti, you are wonderful stuff!

Age: Ps—Grade 2

Books

- Cocca-Leffler, Maryann. *Wednesday is Spaghetti Day.* Scholastic, 1989.
- Hines, Anna. *Daddy Makes the Best Spaghetti.* Clarion, 1986.
- Scwartz, Joel. *The Great Spaghetti Showdown.* Dell, 1988.
- Wilson, Sarah. *Muskrat, Muskrat, Eat Your Peas.* Simon & Schuster, 1989.

Film: *Strega Nona.* Weston Woods, 1977, 9 min.

Activities

Cook up some different types of pasta for the children to taste. Get some of these types of pasta: elbow, ziti, seashell, tubetti, rigatoni, fusilli, linguine, spaghetti, vermicelli. Show the pasta to the children and tell them the names.

Listen to some Italian music such as "Capriccio Italian" by Tchaikovsky. While the music is playing, use uncooked pasta to:

- Make their initials from pasta
- Make pasta collages

All you need for this is paper, pasta and glue.

Sing the song "On Top of Spaghetti" from *Eye Winker, Tom Tinker, Chin Chopper* by Tom Glazer, Doubleday, 1982.

Craft: Spaghetti weaving. You need one package of spaghetti, white glue, construction paper, watercolor markers, large bowl. Follow the instructions on the pasta package but slightly undercook it. Rinse it with cold water, drain it, and put it in the large bowl. Toss a small amount of glue with the spaghetti. Lay a few noodles on the construction paper horizontally and gently press the ends to the paper. Weave a noodle over and under the horizontal noodles and press those ends down also. Weave more noodles and let dry. Add color with the markers. You can also braid the pasta and glue it to a drawing of a face for hair!

Creative Dramatics: Pretend you are uncooked pasta. Throw yourself into the pot start to cook, boil, put yourself on the plate, toss yourself with cheese, wrap yourself around a fork, get chewed, and then be swallowed GULP!

THEME: MORE FOOD IDEAS

A smorgasboard of munchy ideas for your delight.

PROGRAM 1

Age: Ps—Grade 2

Books

- Barbour, Karen. *Little Nino's Pizzeria.* Harper & Row, 1987.
- Numeroff, Laura Joffe. *If You Give a Mouse a Cookie.* Harper & Row, 1985.
- ———. *If You Give a Moose a Muffin.* Harper Collins, 1991.
- O'Keefe, Susan Heyboer. *One Hungry Monster: A Counting Rhyme Book.* Little Brown, 1989.
- Wescott, Nadine. *The Lady With the Alligator Purse.* Joy Street Books, 1988.

Film: *In the Night Kitchen.* Weston Woods, 1987, 6 min.

Fingerplay

Jelly on my head (touch head)
Jelly on my toes (touch toes)
Jelly on my coat (touch coat)
Jelly on my nose (touch nose)
Jelly is my favorite food (rub stomach)
And when I'm in a jelly mood
I can't ever get enough of that yummy jelly stuff!

Fingerplay

Sam, Sam the Pizza Man, put a pizza in a pan
(hold hands out flat in front of you)
He put five pepperonis up on top
(place five pepperonis with fingers)
And cooked it till it was nice and hot,
(wiggle fingers)
And it smelled so yummy, yummy
(sniff air)
It wound up in my tummy, tummy!
(rub stomach)

Craft: Paper pizzas: Each child needs a paper plate and some glue. Also provide the following things to glue on to the paper plate: large red circles for tomato sauce, small orange circles for pepperoni, yellow yarn for grated cheese, brown mushroom shapes. The circles and other shapes should be cut beforehand from construction paper.

Craft: Chef's Hat Collage. You need one chef's hat shape cut from white constuction paper, (see Pattern 17), various vegetable shapes cut from construction paper, glue. The children glue the vegetables on their hats. Ask them what recipe they would like to create and write it on their hats for them.

PATTERN 17

Chef's Hat Collage

Fingerplay

Five little mice on the pantry floor
This little mouse hid behind the door,
This little mouse nibbled on some cheese,
This little mouse gave a little sneeze,
This little mouse ate a piece of cake,
This little mouse not a sound did make,
Then all the little mice, "Squeak" they cried,
And they found a hole and ran inside!

Hold fingers down on top of other palm, then wiggle each one at a time. To make the mice run in the hole, run fingers up and under arm.

Activity: Peanut Butter Playdough. After sharing the counting story *One Hungry Monster*, make Peanut Butter Playdough. You need peanut butter, nonfat dry milk, a large bowl, forks, spoons, and butter knives, waxed paper. Mix equal parts of peanut butter and nonfat dry milk in the bowl. Use the dough as playdough, working with it on top of waxed paper. Encourage the children to create hungry monsters with peanut butter on their lips just like the book.

Music: "Peanut Butter" from *Camels, Cats & Rainbows* by Paul Straussman, Gentle Wind, GW 1009. Or, sing "Peanut Butter and Jelly:"

> First you take the peanuts and you smash 'em, smash 'em, smash 'em, smash 'em, smash 'em
> *Chorus:* Peanut, peanut butter and jelly, peanut, peanut butter and jelly.
> Then you take the peanuts and you spread 'em, spread 'em, spread 'em, spread 'em, spread 'em.
> *Chorus*
> Then you take the peanuts and you eat 'em, eat 'em, eat 'em, eat 'em, eat 'em.
> *Chorus*

Resource: Playful Puppets, has "Puppets That Swallow" that could be used with storytimes about food or eating. They have bears, caterpillars, cookie eaters, pigs, etc. that all swallow. prices range from $18 to $150. Address: 9002 Stoneleigh Court, Fairfax, VA, 22031, (703) 280-5070.

PROGRAM 2

Age: Grades 3 and up

Books

- Dahl, Roald. *Rhyme Stew*. Viking, 1990.
- Delton, Judy. *Cookies and Crutches*. Dell, 1988.
- Elish, Dan. *The Worldwide Dessert Contest*. Orchard, 1988.
- Pinkwater, Daniel. *Fat Men From Space*. Dodd Mead, 1977.
- *The Please Touch Cookbook*. Silver Press, 1990.

Activity: Bubbly raisins. Put raisins in the bottom of a glass and pour light colored soda such as ginger ale over them. The raisins will (magically) rise to the top of the glass because of the bubbles. Say a few magic words as you do this. Invite the kids to do the trick also, but give them flat ginger ale and it won't work! Let them guess how the trick is done, and then serve raisins!

Activity: Fortune cookies. Buy a bag of fortune cookies. Have the children write their own fortunes on strips of paper.

Activity: Design placemats or menus. First brainstorm a menu or placemat for your favorite book character. What might he eat? For example, *James and the Giant Peach*, Roald Dahl (Knopf, 1961), might have peach pie, peach preserves, peach pancakes, and eat off of a giant menu covered with Ps! Cut magazine pictues out and use them to decorate your menus and placemats.

THEME: APPLES

Everyone's favorite fruit.

Age: Ps—Grade 2

Opening song: Sing this song to the tune of "The Muffin Man."

> Do you know the apple man, the apple man, the apple man
> Do you know the apple man, who lives on Orange lane?
> Yes I know the apple man, the apple man, the apple man,
> Yes I know the apple man who lives on Orange lane.
> Oh, he plants his seeds in spring, seeds in spring, seeds in spring, Oh he plants his seeds in spring down by Orange lane. (Make up more verses.)

Books

- Caseley, Judith. *Apple Pie and Onions*. Greenwillow, 1987.
- Hogrogian, Nonny. *Apple Tree! Apple Tree!* Children's, 1983.

PATTERN 18

Apple Prints Tree

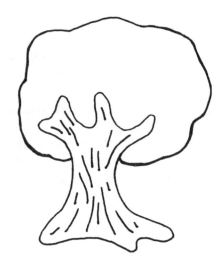

PATTERN 19

Apple Book

- Kellogg, Steven. *Johnny Appleseed.* Morrow Junior Books, 1988.
- Micucci, Charles. *The Life and Times of the Apple Tree.* Orchard, 1992.
- Scheer, Julian. *Rain Makes Apple Sauce.* Holiday House, 1964.

Film: *The Legend of Johnny Appleseed.* 20 minutes, 1966, Demco.

Fingerplay

Here is an apple tree with leaves so green.
  (Make a tree shape holding your arms up high)
Here are the apples that hang in between.
  (Clench fists)
When the wind blows, the apples fall.
  (Wave arms as if wind is blowing, lower fists)
Here is a basket to gather them all.
  (Make circle with arms for basket)

Craft: Apple prints. You need large corks, tree shapes (see Pattern 18) cut from green construction paper, margerine tubs filled with a little red poster paint. (Corks can be obtained from arts and crafts stores.) Give each child a tree shape and a cork. They dip the corks in the red paint and then press them on the paper to print apples on their trees.

Craft: Apple books. Cut red construction paper into an apple shape. Use Pattern 19. Cut several white pages into the same shape. Punch a hole in them and tie them together with yarn. Make a book by writing down the stories or poems the children tell you about apples. You could also make one of these for each child to take home.

Flannel Board: Use Patterns 20, 21 and 22 to make a flannel board for the story *Turtle Tale,* Frank Asch, Dial, 1978.

Finishing Touches: As a final activity, cut out small apple shapes from red construction paper and attach them with scotch tape to the children's noses! Let them pretend to be apples: On the tree, being picked, being polished, and "CRUNCH", being eaten!

PATTERNS 20, 21 and 22

Turtle Tale Flannel Board

Music: "Johnny Appleseed" from *Storysinger* by Chris Holder, Gentle Winds, GW1014.

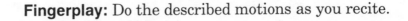

THEME: BREAKFAST TIME

Invite kids to breakfast at the library. Serve toaster waffles, or have a pancake eating contest. Ask your local Jaycees or other civic group to sponsor a pancake breakfast for members of the reading club. Call the program "Breakfast of Champion Readers."

Age: Ps—Grade 2

Books

- Carle, Eric. *Pancakes, Pancakes.* Knopf, 1970.
- Cauley, Lorinda. *The Pancake Boy: An Old Norwegian Folktale.* Putnam, 1988.
- Ginsburg, Mirra. *The Night It Rained Pancakes.* Greenwillow, 1980.
- Gullikson, Sandy. *Trouble for Breakfast.* Dial, 1990.

Films

- *The Emperor's Oblong Pancake.* Sterling, 1963, 6 min.
- *Waffles.* Churchill, 1985, 11 min.

Fingerplay: Do the described motions as you recite.

Mix a pancake,
Stir a pancake,
Pop it in the pan,
Fry the pancake,
Toss the pancake,
Catch it if you can!

Christina Rosetti, *Sing Song,* 1871.

Craft: Pancake Man puppet. You need brown construction paper, spring type clothes pins, black markers, glue, scissors. Cut a circle out of the construction paper. Cut the circle in half,

FIGURE 3-1

Pancake Man Puppet

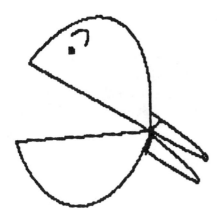

making the top a little larger than the bottom. Glue the top half to the side of the top of a spring type clothespin. Glue the bottom half of the circle to the side of the bottom of the clothespin. Draw an eye on the top half with the marker. To make the puppet talk, squeeze the clothespin open and shut.

Fingerplay

Five little donuts in a breakfast shop,
Sprinkled with powdered sugar on top,
Along comes (insert name of child) with a penny to pay,
He/she buys a donut and takes it away.

(continue with 4, 3, 2, 1, using different children's names)

Song to sing: "The King's Breakfast" from *The Pooh Song Book*, page 93, by A.A. Milne. (Dutton, 1961)

THEME: CHOCOLATE

There are always lots of chocoholics at the library! Watch out—some may sneak their own private supply with them!

Age: Grades 3 and up

Books

- Adoff, Arnold. *Chocolate Dreams*. Lothrop, 1989.
- Catling, Patrick. *The Chocolate Touch*. Morrow, 1979.
- Dineen, Jacqueline. *Chocolate*. Carolrhoda, 1991.
- Howe, James. *Hot Fudge*. Morrow, 1989.
- Smith, Robert K. *Chocolate Fever*. Dell, 1979.

Chocolate Facts:

- Hernando Cortés, the Spanish explorer brought chocolate back from Mexico in the 1500s.
- The Aztec Indians of Mexico gave chocolate to Cortés. It came from a tree they called kakahuatl, now called cacao.

· Hershey, Pennsylvania smells like chocolate; it is the home of Hershey's Candy Factory.
· The average family in the United States eats about 11 pounds of chocolate a year.
· All of these things have been made from chocolate: a jigsaw puzzle, a chess set, the statue of liberty!

Activity: Dramatize some poetry from *Chocolate Dreams* by Adoff or present the play version of *Charlie and the Chocolate Factory* as adapted by Richard George. (Knopf, 1976)

Unwrap some artistic talents by having a candy wrapper contest. Pass out index cards and cover them with aluminum foil. Now cut a piece of white paper to wrap around it like a candy wrapper. Design the wrappers, then glue them around the foil. Use book characters or titles for inspirations for the names of the candy wrapper designs, such as "Ramona's Raisin Chocolate Bar" for Ramona Quimby. Display them in a basket in the children's department.

Demonstration: Make your own chocolate bar. You need 2 tablespoons of powdered cocoa, 2 tablespoons of sugar, 1 tablespoon of butter, a double boiler, wax paper. Put enough water in the bottom of the boiler to just touch the top half and boil. Turn off the the heat, put the cocoa, sugar, and butter into the top and stir until the mixture is smooth and melted. Spread the wax paper over the counter. Carefully remove the top of the boiler and pour the chocolate mixture onto the wax paper. Let it harden, and taste.

PATTERN 23

Chocolate Kiss Bulletin Board Shape

Bulletin Board Idea: Using Pattern 23 cut chocolate kisses out of brown construction paper. Wrap the kisses in aluminum foil and attach tissue paper strips to the kisses, like the strip on a real chocolate kiss. Write the titles of good books on the strips. Partially unwrap some of these kisses, and then hang them on a bulletin board with the caption "Unwrap a Good Book. . . .How Sweet It Is!"

More poems to share

· "Chocolate Cake" in *All the Day Long* by Nina Payne, Atheneum, 1973.

- "Chocolate Milk" and "Fudge" in *Rainy, Rainy Saturday* by Jack Prelutsky, Greenwillow, 1980.
- "The Reason I Like Chocolate" in *Vacation Time* by Nikki Giovanni, Morrow, 1980.

THEME: FOOD FUN

Age: Grades 3 and up

Books

- Conford, Ellen. *What's Cooking, Jenny Archer?* Little Brown, 1990.
- Kline, Suzy. *Orp and the Chop Suey Burgers.* Putnam, 1990.
- Naylor, Phyllis Reynolds. *Beetles Lightly Toasted.* Atheneum, 1987.
- Pryor, Bonnie. *Vinegar, Pancakes, and Vanishing Cream.* Morrow, 1987.

Film: *The Doughnuts.* Weston Woods, 1964, 26 min.

Activity: Tell the story "A Whale of a Tale," pages 1-6, from *Twenty Tellable Tales*, Margaret Read MacDonald, H.W. Wilson, 1986.

Have the kids write a letter to the food they hate the most!

Beetles: Read aloud from *Beetles Lightly Toasted.* Then make beetles. You need cleaned out walnut shell halves, poster paint, clear nail polish, glue, scissors, pipe cleaners, felt, paper scraps, magnetic tape (from the craft store), wiggly craft eyes (small). Paint the walnut halves an appropriate color for your bug. After the paint dries, seal it with nail polish. Add eyes, legs (pipe cleaners), antennae, etc. Cut a piece of felt to fit the bottom of the shell. Glue the magnetic tape on the back of the felt. You now have a magnet for the refrigerator.

Foody Riddles

I'm round and pink, with fuzz on my cheeks.
What am I? A Peach!
I'm plum cute. What am I? A Plum!
If you cut me, I'll make you cry. What am I? An Onion!

SUGGESTIONS FOR A READERS' THEATER

- "Hershele Gets A Meal," pp. 166-168 or "In Which Tigger Comes to the Forest and Has Breakfast," pp. 174-188, from the book *Presenting Reader's Theater* Caroline Feller Bauer, H.W. Wilson, 1987.
- *The Day Jimmy's Boa Ate the Wash.* Trinka H. Noble. Dial, 1980.
- A story to dramatize: *Mister Cat-and-a-Half.* Richard Pervear, Macmillan, 1986.

RELATED ACTIVITIES

COOKBOOK BOOKTALKS AND DISPLAYS

Use some of these cookbooks taken from storybook beginnings to make a display or booktalk:

- Anderson, Gretchen. *Louisa May Alcott Cookbook.* Little Brown, 1981.
- Bayley, Monica. *Wonderful Wizard of Oz Cookbook.* Macmillan, 1981.
- Blain, Diane. *The Boxcar Children Cookbook.* Albert Whitman, 1990.
- Boxer, Arabella. *The Wind in the Willows Country Cookbook.* Scribner, 1983.
- Dobrin, Arnold. *Peter Rabbit's Natural Food Cookbook.* Warner, 1977.
- Ellison, Virginia H. *The Pooh Cookbook.* Dutton, 1969.
- Keene, Carolyn. *The Nancy Drew Cookbook.* Grossett and Dunlap, 1973.
- Lane, Margaret. *The Beatrix Potter Country Cookery Book.* Warne, 1982.

- Macdonald, Kate. *The Anne of Green Gables Cookbook.* Oxford University Press, 1985.
- Travers, P.L. *Mary Poppins in the Kitchen.* HBJ, 1975.
- Walker, Barbara. *The Little House Cookbook.* Harper and Row, 1979.

COMMUNITY PARTNERSHIPS

Invite a senior citizens group to your library. Have the library kids provide home cooked refreshments. The seniors can bring their recipes for the children to illustrate.

TAKE HOME ACTIVITY SHEETS

Reproduce the following directions for the children to do at home.

Snack Food Sculpture: You need bread sticks, pretzels, rippled potato chips, corn chips, cheese curls, crackers, cream cheese, sour cream, 1 pkg. dried onion soup mix, mixing bowl, mixing spoon, plastic knife for each child, paper plate for each child.

Mix the cream cheese with the sour cream, then blend in the soup mix. This will be your paste. Using the paste, each child creates a sculpture out of the snack foods. Start with crackers or potato chips as bases. Use pretzels and bread sticks as frameworks. Display the finished sculptures before eating them. Give out prizes such as The Jelly Bean Award for the funniest looking sculpture.

Pizza geography: Use your favorite homemade pizza dough recipe or buy a can of ready made dough or crust mix. While the dough rises, look through a geography book and think about foods from different countries. Pick out a map to make from pizza. Preheat the oven according to your directions. Now flatten out your dough and form it into the shape of the map you choose. Put on tomato sauce, and add toppings to decorate your map. Mark various cities with olives. Mark mountains with mushrooms. Fill in bodies of water with cheese. Bake your pizza according to directions. Take a picture of the finished product before you eat!

Food Faces: You need bread slices, peanut butter or cheese spread; radishes, grapes, or cherry tomatoes for eyes; carrot sticks cucumber slices, or cheese chunks for noses; avocado, apple, or orange slices for mouths; bean sprouts, celery leaves, or lettuce for hair; knives, plates, napkins.

Slice up all the vegetables and fruits and assemble on platters. Put out the bread and spreads. Begin creating food faces on the bread: the spread acts as glue. Have a contest for the yuckiest face, etc. After you are done, eat them!

Bread Painting: You need; 2 slices of white bread, assorted food coloring, 2 quarts of milk, paper cups, cotton swabs, toaster. Fill the paper cups with milk and add a little food coloring to them. Use different cotton swabs for each color. Now create works of art on the bread canvas with food coloring paint. Dry the bread in the toaster set for very light. If possible, take pictures of these creations for display before eating them.

4

Your Library: A place to look for new ideas and to examine theories about animals, machines, space, and time.

THEME: ZOO

Zookeeper for a day!

Age: Ps—Grade 2

Books

- Asch, Frank. *Monkey Face.* Parents Magazine Press, 1977.
- Bottner, Barbara. *Zoo Song.* Scholastic, 1987.
- Ehlert, Lois. *Color Zoo.* Lippincott, 1989.
- Kitchen, Burt. *Gorilla-Chinchilla.* Dial, 1990.
- Lopshire, Robert. *Put Me in the Zoo.* Random House, 1960.

Chalk Board Story: The book *Monkey Face* by Asch works well as a chalk board story. Simply draw the picture the baby monkey draws of his mother on the chalkboard and add the features he adds as he meets his friends.

Fingerplay

Five little monkeys, sitting on the door,
One fell off and then there were four.
Four little monkeys, sitting in a tree,
One fell out and then there were three.
Three little monkeys going to the zoo,
One got lost and then there were two.
Two little monkeys having lots of fun,
One ran away and then there was one.
One little monkey sitting in the sun
He ate a banana, then there were none.

73

Activity: Spots Day. Use the age old favorite story *Put Me in the Zoo* and have a Spots Day! Play put-the-spots-on game. Enlarge the creature from the story and make various colored circles for dots. Play like pin the tail on the donkey. Serve M & M's. Get some sticker dots of various colors and stick them on the children. You might want to pass out invitations for this the week before and tell all the kids to wear something with polka dots on it.

Film: *If I Ran the Zoo.* Filmstrip or VHS, Communication Skills, Inc.

PATTERN 24

Gorilla-Chinchilla

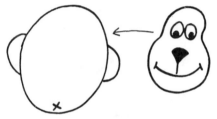

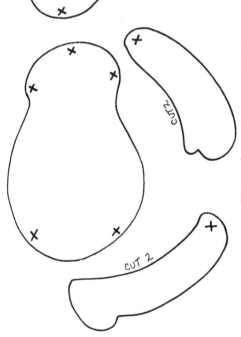

Song: "Going to the Zoo" by Tom Paxton, from *The Raffi Singable Songbook,* Crown, 1980, pp. 32-33.

Activity: Gorillas. Use the book *Gorilla-Chinchilla.* You need gorilla Pattern 24, scissors, brads, tape, crayons. Cut out the patterns and color with crayons. Glue the gorilla's face on and draw eyes, nose, and mouth. Attach the gorilla parts together with brads at the X's. Tape on a piece of yellow yarn as a tail.

THEME: SHADOWS

Shadows and shadowplay are a fascinating science concept.

Age: Ps—Grade 2

Books

- Asch, Frank. *Bear Shadow.* Prentice Hall, 1985.
- Cendrars, Blaise. *Shadows.* Scribners, 1982.
- Mahy, Margaret. *The Boy With Two Shadows.* Lippincott, 1987.
- Narahashi, Keiko. *I Have a Friend.* M. K. McElderry, 1987.
- Tompert, Anne. *Nothing Sticks Like a Shadow.* Houghton Mifflin, 1984.

PATTERN 25

Shadow Shapes

Rhyme

I have a friend
He goes where I go
I have a friend
His name is shadow.

Activity: Shadow box. You need a box at least 18 × 24-inches, such as a shirt box. Cut three openings in the box: a 12 × 12-inch hole on the top and bottom, and one 4 × 4-inch hole near the bottom on a short end. Tape or staple over one of the the 12 × 12-inch holes with white fabric such as a sheet. Place your light source (such as a slide or filmstrip projector) at the 4 × 4-inch hole. Use some of the shapes in Pattern 25 to make shadow puppets from cardboard. Tape them on to sticks or straws and hold them behind the large hole without the fabric. Act out a story using the shadows; let the children try too! You can also use your shadow puppets with an overhead projector.

Activity: Shadow Shapes. You need butcher paper, tacks or masking tape, assorted markers and crayons, slide projector. Tack or tape a large piece of paper to a wall. Plug the slide projector in and aim it at the paper. Turn off the other lights. The children get partners and take turns tracing each other's shadows on the butcher paper. Make sure you have enough paper so everyone can trace at once. Tell the children to move around and try to create funny shadows to trace. Tell them it is okay to overlap the shadows. The slide projector can be moved around to enlarge or shrink shadows also. Turn on the lights. Children now color in their shadows with patterns, stars, dots, stripes, checks, and solid colors. Tell them to fill in overlapping shapes with contrasting colors or patterns. Diplay this as a bulletin board with the caption "The Shadow's Not the Only One Who Knows at the Library!"

Activity: Shadow tracings. You need white construction paper, small objects such as a vase, book, can, and crayons. On a sunny day, have the children sit by a window. Put each object by the window on a piece of white construction paper. Have the children trace the objects' shadows with the crayons. With several of the tracings, play a matching game for the shadow and the real object.

THEME: BALLOONS

Balloons float and so will the child's imagination.

Age: Ps—Grade 2

Books

- Brunhoff, Jean de. *The Travels of Babar*. Random House, 1934.
- Calhoun, Mary. *Hot Air Henry*. Morrow, 1981.
- Wade, Alan. *I'm Flying*. Knopf, 1990.
- Wildsmith, Brian. *Bear's Adventure*. Pantheon, 1981.
- Willard, Nancy. *The Well Mannered Balloon*. Harcourt Brace World, 1979.

Film: *Curious George*. Churchill, 1984, 14 min.

Idea: Celebrate Balloon Day—August 17.

Balloon Dancing: Have the children pretend to be balloons. Let them lie flat on the floor and begin to blow themselves up. The children slowly begin to stand and make blowing sounds. Then the children can "float" around. They can also dramatize being blown by winds, caught in a tree, and then popping and collapsing.

Fingerplay

> One balloon floats up high
> Until it can touch the sky;
> One balloon is in a tree,
> It is yellow, I can see,
> The next balloon is on the ground
> Where it bounces all around.
> The last balloon, you understand,
> Is right here tied around my hand!

Activities: Balloon's Eye View. Have the children think about what it would be like to travel by balloon. Let them draw pictures of what the world would look like from the sky—

people would be tiny dots, the ground would look like a patchwork quilt. (For ages 5 and up.)

Ask the children to finish the following sentence "If I could float and fly high like a balloon I would travel to . . ."

Use a book such as *Dr. Dropo's Balloon Sculptures for Beginners* (Bruce Fife, Java Publications, 1988) and make some balloon sculptures while the children watch.

THEME: TIME TRAVEL

There are many books about time travel to use for a discover the library booktalk.

Age: Grades 3 and up

Books

- Bellairs, John. *Trolley to Yesterday*. Dial, 1989.
- Conrad, Pam. *Stonewords*. Harper & Row, 1990.
- Hahn, Mary Downing. *The Doll in the Garden*. Clarion, 1989.
- Pfeffer, Susan Beth. *Rewind to Yesterday*. Delacorte, 1988.

Activity: Discuss the concept of time. Ask the children what time is. Let the children form small groups and brainstorm about inventions to come. What food will we eat in the future, what clothes, what transportation? Use the story starter "I was riding my _____ to school dressed in my new _____ in the fall of the year 2037."

THEME: SPACE

Aliens visit the library—watch out, they could be next to YOU!

Age: Grades 3 and Up

Books

- Deem, James. *How to Catch a Flying Saucer.* Houghton, 1991.
- Etra, Jonahan. *Aliens for Breakfast.* Random House, 1988.
- Gormley, Beatrice. *Wanted: UFO.* Dutton, 1990.
- Sant, Thomas. *The Amazing Adventures of Albert and His Flying Machine.* Dutton Lodestar, 1990.

Game: Flying saucer fun. Cut out five cardboard circles about 5-inches in diameter. Decorate to look like flying saucers and number each from 1 to 5. Place a piece of string across the floor. Stand about four feet from the string, toss the saucers across the string. Add up the numbers of the saucers that land right side up beyond the string with the number showing. Play to see who gets the highest score in the same number of tosses.

PATTERN 26

Jello-Box Rocket

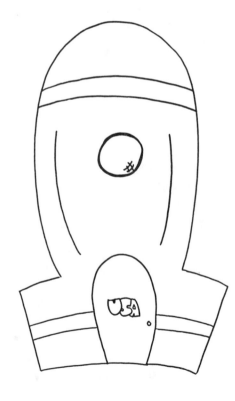

Craft: Super Saucers. You need two plastic bowls, two pipe cleaners, glue, and markers. Glue the two bowls together mouth to mouth. Decorate the bowls after the glue dries to look like spaceships. Poke a small hole in the top and add the pipe cleaners as antennae.

Craft: Jello Box Spaceships. You need Pattern 26, scissors, glue, crayons, and empty jello boxes. Copy one pattern for each child and give each a jello box. With the box on its end, cut a door in the longer side. Now cut out your pattern and cut the door so it opens and closes. Color the rocket and glue to the box so the door is over the hole you cut. Your rocket is ready to ride!

Craft: Alien Flakes. Decorate some cereal boxes to look like "Alien Flakes" as found in the book *Aliens for Breakfast.* Cover the boxes with white paper and color with crayons. You might also suggest types of cereals for different characters from other space stories, such as for Mrs. Piggle Wiggle in *Mrs. Piggle Wiggle on the Moon.*

THEME: COMPUTERS AND MACHINES

Computer games are a familiar pastime as more kids become computer literate.

Age: Grades 3 and up

Books

- Chetwin, Grace. *Out of the Dark World.* Lothrop, Lee, and Shepherd, 1985.
- D'Ignazio, Fred. *Chip Mitchell and the Case of the Chocolate Covered Bugs.* Dutton, 1985.
- Landsman, Sandy. *The Gadget Factor.* Atheneum, 1984.
- Macaulay, David. *The Way Things Work.* Houghton Mifflin, 1988
- VanVelde, Vivian. *User Unfriendly.* HBJ, 1991.

Activities

Ask a local computer store to come and demonstrate their computers, or have a computer club do this. There are lots of computer user interest groups around.

Discuss how computers work. Talk about books that have the theme of computers taking over. Many movies have this theme also.

Craft: Create your own computer or machine. Ask the kids to first brainstorm about what kind of machine or computer it will be, what it will do, how it will operate. Encourage them to be really imaginative and computerize things like skateboards, washing machines, etc.

Each child needs scissors, markers, a cardboard box the right size for the proposed machine, and plastic sandwich wrap for "glass." Each child should then draw knobs, lights, buttons, and switches. If their machine speaks, then a tape recorder could be placed inside with a child-made recording of a machine like voice. Any moving parts or windows can be cut out. (The librarian may need to do this carefully with a sharp knife) Cover the windows with "glass" by taping the plastic wrap to the inside over the opening.

THEME: ROCKS

Rockhunt at the library.

Age: All ages.

Books

- Alcock, Vivian. *Stonewalkers*. Delacorte, 1983.
- Goble, Paul. *Iktomi and the Boulder*. Orchard, 1988.
- Kreiger, David. *Too Many Stones*. Young Scott Books, 1970.
- Stolz, Mary. *Zekmet the Stonecarver*. Harcourt, 1988.
- Yolen, Jane. *Dove Isabeau*. Harcourt, 1988.

Start by telling or reading some of the following tales and poems: "The Stone" from *The Foundling and Other Tales of Prydain* by Lloyd Alexander (Holt, 1973); "Beach Stone" in *These Small Stones* Norma Farber, ed. (Harper, 1987); or "The Perilous Voyage Homeward" in *Classic Myths to Read Aloud* by Scylla and Charybdis (Crown, 1989).

Activity: Pet Rocks. Bring in rocks to examine or a rock collection for display. Give each child a rock to take home and encourage them to think of it as a pet, giving it a name and caring for it.

Activity: Stone Writing. Ask the children to think what it would be like to have a magic stone, such as the one in "The Stone." Ask them to write a short story or poem about their magic stone. Or, have them write about what it might be like to be turned into stone—as in *The Stonewalkers*—or to carve a stone. For a more novel idea, gather some flat stones, and have the children write poems about stones and rocks on them using permanent markers.

Craft: Rock Sculpture. Collect a variety of small rocks and cardboard. Let the children glue the rocks in freeform shapes to the cardboard to create sculptures.

Fingerplay

> Five little rocks, sitting on the floor,
> One rolled away, then there were four.
> Four little rocks, floating in the sea,
> One sank down, and then there were three.
> Three little rocks, inside my shoe,
> I took one out, and then there were two.
> Two little rocks, pick them up for fun,
> One was dropped, then there was one.
> One little rock left in my hand,
> I held it too long and it turned to sand.

THEME: ECOLOGY

Age: Grades 3 and Up

Books

- Elkington, Julia Hailes, and Joel Makower. *Going Green: A Kids Guide to Saving the Planet.* Puffin, 1990
- Haines, Gail. *Micromysteries: Stories of Scientific Detection.* Dodd/Putnam, 1988.
- McLaughlin, Molly. *Earthworms, Dirt, and Rotten Leaves: An Exploration of Ecology.* Atheneum, 1986.
- Pearce, Fred. *The Big Green Book.* Kingfisher Books, 1991.
- Wilkes, Angela. *My First Green Book.* Knopf, 1991.

Activities

Using the book *Going Green,* get your library kids to participate in any of the following projects, or others described in other environmental books:

- Recycling.
- Creating an organic garden.
- Choosing and campaigning for environmentally safe products.
- Campaigning against aerosols.
- Testing for acid rain.
- Cutting down on excess household garbage.

Obtain Demco's "The Precious Earth" catalog for books, kits, activities and other materials with an ecological theme. Address: Demco, Box 7488, Madison, WI 53707. 1-800-356-1200.

THEME: MOON AND STARS

Age: Ps—Grade 2

Books

- Berger, Barbara. *Grandfather Twilight.* Philomel, 1984.
- Rice, Eve. *City Night.* Greenwillow, 1987.
- Ryan, Cheli Duran. *Hildilid's Night.* Macmillan, 1971.
- Thaler, Mike. *The Moon and the Balloon.* Hastings, 1982.

Films

- *Moon Man.* Weston Woods, 1981, 8 min.
- *Happy Birthday, Moon.* Weston Woods, 1985, 7 min.

Opening: Do some star gazing at the library. Use the story *Grandfather Twilight.* Let the children tell you their own story about Grandmother Sunrise. What kind of jewel might she have in her chest? Give them plastic or wooden beads, their own "jewels" to take home.

Activities

Serve moon cookies. Bake or buy large round, white sugar cookies. If you have time, decorate with raisins to make faces for the "moons" (use peanut butter to make the raisins stick).

Use the story from *The Moon and the Balloon* as a flannel board. Enlarge the drawings onto vellum and cut out. Use a real yellow balloon as the deflated balloon: simply tape it to the flannel board.

Use a story such as *Hildilid's Night*. Then make a wishing star. Cover a star with foil and tell the children it's a wishing star. Let them pass it around and take turns wishing. Next ask the children how they would get rid of the night as Hildilid tried to in the story.

Rhyme

Here are stars in the night
Watch them twinkle with their light
When you see them shining bright
Make a wish with all your might.

Craft: Glitter Stars. You need glitter, wax paper, and a white craft glue that dries hard. Pass out wax paper to each child. Use a glue bottle with a pointed tip to draw star shapes on the wax paper. Sprinkle them with glitter, making sure the glue is completely covered. Let the stars dry for 48 hours, and then carefully peel them off the wax paper.

RELATED ACTIVITIES

Hold a mini science or idea fair in your library. Invite library kids and their parents to come up with inventions or projects and write them up with illustrations. Make a display of these, encouraging Rube Goldberg-like ideas. Give out ribbons and display them in the children's department.

You can promote the fun of science by demonstrating how to make a volcano. You need an empty flowerpot placed upside down in a large baking pan, an empty can (such as a tuna fish can) with one end removed, a paper cup with the bottom cut off placed upside down on the tuna can, scissors, masking tape,

FIGURE 4-1

A Chemical Volcano

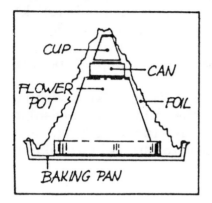

foil, spoons, 1/2 cup vinegar, baking soda, red food coloring, and dishwashing detergent. Put the paper cup on top of the flower pot, cover the structure with crumpled tin foil. Cut an X in the top of the foil and fold it down inside the cup to form the volcano hole. Add a spoonful of baking soda and a spoonful of dishwashing detergent to the tuna can through the top hole. Measure out the vinegar in another container and add some food coloring to it. Start the volcano by pouring the vinegar/food coloring solution into the tuna can.

Sponsor a "Come as Your Favorite Character" Party. Ask the children to dress like their favorite scientific or literary character. Let them tell about themselves as the character or read aloud from their character's story.

COMMUNITY PARTNERSHIP

Invite local science fair winners to come and display their projects. Do a program where they tell about how they came up with their idea, how they felt when they won, etc.

TAKE HOME ACTIVITY SHEETS

Reproduce the following activites for the children to do at home.

Magic Squares: You need a sheet of acetate, masking tape, vaseline, oil paints, poster paints, turpentine, and scissors. Cut two 4-inch squares of acetate. Smear some vaseline along the edges of the squares. Mix some poster paint with water and thin the oil paints with turpentine. Put a few drops of one color poster paint and one color oil paint on one of the squares. Lay the other acetate square on top of it and tape them together with masking tape. Hold your magic square up to the light and bend or squeeze. The colors will not mix, but will form beautiful patterns.

Magic egg: You need a hard-boiled egg and an uncooked egg. Hand the two eggs to a friend and announce that you can tell the cooked one from the raw one without cracking the shell.

Put one egg at a time on a table and spin it. If it spins fast, then crack it open on your head—it is the hard boiled one. If it spins slowly and stops quickly, don't crack it open—it is the raw one. The secret to this magic is in the spin. The hard boiled egg is solid and spins as a unit. In a raw egg you spin the shell, but the shell has to start moving the liquid insides. This uses up the energy of the spin and the egg spins slowly.

5 PUBLICITY AND PROMOTION

Promoting programs is almost as important as the planning process. Children won't attend even the most wonderful program if they aren't aware of it. For your Reading Club Programs and related activities, you might want to develop a media kit that provides information about the events and includes:

- Press releases
- A schedule of events
- A feature story about the reading clubs
- PSA tags (Public Service Announcements)
- Letters for newspapers, schools, city officials about the events.

Ask local restaurants to use paper placemats with the reading club theme imprinted on them. Do the same about grocery sacks for local stores. A local printer might donate the printing of these or other reading club materials.

Other types of publicity for your reading club include billboards, bus billboard advertising, and free bus rides for children presenting library cards. Use posters, bookmarks, and flyers to publicize your program. Distribute them in day care centers, schools, banks, Y's, churches, restaurants, grocery stores, and any other place children and their parents might see them. Some sample press releases are provided. Adapt these to fit your needs.

TIP

Name your reading club with a catchy title and insert this where the PSA says "reading club."

COMMUNICATION TOOLS

SAMPLE PRESS RELEASE

The (Your Library's Name) Reading Clubs for children of all ages! (Your library's name) will sponsor a reading club to

TIPS ON WRITING PUBLICITY RELEASES:

- Double space all releases
- Limit to one page
- Write short, concise paragraphs
- Include all essential information: who, what, where, when, why, and how
- Do not assume the reader knows anything about the library
- Include hours, phone number, and location
- Attach a flyer to your news release

promote reading and fun. The reading club begins on (date). So come to the library and sign up for the Read to Me club for non-reading children, or the Reading Club for readers. Fun-filled activities are scheduled during the (insert # of weeks) weeks of the Library's reading club. The following is a schedule of events and programs at the (you library's name). (Here include a list or calendar of events) Call (phone number) for more information.

SAMPLE PSA (PUBLIC SERVICE ANNOUNCEMENT FOR THE RADIO)
:20 Seconds

Be a happy reader. . .at the library! Come to the (name) library and check out the Reading Clubs.

The theme for this club is (insert your theme or club title here) The library will offer different types of activities to promote reading and fun. Just come to the (name) library beginning (date).

So be a happy reader at the (name) library.

A public service message from the (name) library and this station.

SCHOOL VISITS

An important way to publicize the reading club at your library is through school visits. Schools and teachers are natural allies to work with in attracting children to reading during the summer. Cooperate with them in any way possible.

Try to arrange as many visits as possible to elementary schools in your area in the spring. Once you schedule your summer programs and have publicity in hand you can begin these visits. This is a great case for advance planning! Contact your school district's administrative office and ask permission to promote the library's summer reading programs. Schedule the visits through principals, teachers, or school librarians. Take bookmarks, posters and any program flyers you produce. Dress up like a camper complete with a backpack full of riddles, jokes, and stories relating to the theme. Promote your library's programs and then leave a poster as a reminder with the beginning date of your reading club written on it. Ask the school librarian to display it in a prominent spot. Some schools will even include reading club flyers in end of the year report cards.

SAMPLE LETTER TO SCHOOL

Dear Teachers and Administrators,

The (Your Library's Name) is pleased to announce the Reading Club for children—(insert your theme or club name)

The purpose of (insert club theme or name) is to promote reading and stimulate curiosity and attract children to the library. The emphasis is on having fun with books.

(Insert club name) is a reading club where children keep track of the reading they do. Children may register for these programs beginning (date).

Many activities are also planned at the library to highlight this year's theme. A staff member of our library would be glad to visit your school and tell the students about the reading club.

We need your help! Encourage students to visit the public library and sign up for the Reading Club this summer and enjoy (insert theme or name)

Sincerely,

Your Name
Title

SAMPLE FOLLOW UP LETTER TO SCHOOLS

Principal
Elementary School
Your City
Your State

Dear Principal,

Do you know who from your school participated in (insert your club's name) this summer?

(Here list the names of the participants)

These are the children from your school that participated in the Reading Club (insert club's name) We are very proud of them and hope you are, too!

The (your library) offers other programs for children during the school year and summer. We will be available to come to your school in the spring and talk to the children about the next Reading Club. If you are interested please call (phone number) to schedule a visit.

Good Luck to you, your staff, and your students this new school year.

Sincerely,

Your Name.
Title

SAMPLE LETTER TO PARENTS

Dear Parent,

To encourage your child to read this summer, the (your library's name) Library is sponsoring a Reading Club. The theme for this club will be (insert theme), including all kinds of books and activities that promote reading and fun. These programs begin (date) and end (date). Contact this library at (phone number) for a complete schedule of activities planned.

Encourage your child to participate in these reading clubs! By doing so you are helping your child retain hard-earned skills acquired during the school year.

The library has books, cassettes, and videos available for check out. Your family can explore the darkest jungles and the highest mountains with an inexpensive trip to the library! And your library card is free!

See you at the library!

Sincerely,

Your Name
Title

SAMPLE LETTER TO PRESCHOOL/DAYCARE CENTER

Dear Preschool/Daycare Center,

The (your library's name) is pleased to announce (insert club name), the Reading Club theme. Preschool children can participate in these programs by being good listeners as members of the Read-to-Me Club. Chilren who are reading can join (insert club name) and record the books or time they read.

(Your library's name) also provides special programs just for daycare centers. Please contact the library to register for (insert club name) and for information on our special daycare programs.

Please call the library at (Phone Number) for a complete schedule of daycare events at the library.

We are looking forward to making participation in the Reading Clubs an entertaining as well as educational experience.

In addition, please contact the library for information on the following services:

· A library card for your school or daycare.
· Audiovisual Materials such as films, records, videos and filmstrips for checkout.

FIGURE 5-1   Tips for Parents

Your involvement with your child this summer can make all the difference in whether the summer reading program is an exciting adventure or a frustrating disappointment. Here are some ideas to help you make this summer's reading program all that it can and should be for your child.

* **Help your child set a realistic book goal for the summer.** Try to encourage a goal that will challenge the child but not so ambitious that book enjoyment becomes a chore or successful participation too great a challenge.

* **Establish a regular time for reading in your home for all members of the family.**

* **Offer to share stories at bedtime or as dinner conversation.**

* **Encourage your child to share favorite stories with you.**

* **Show genuine interest in the stories or programs your child discovers during the summer.**

* **Appreciate all books the child selects, even the ones that look "too easy".** Summer is a time for fun, after all, and you can always guide your child to a more challenging book the next time you visit the library.

> * **Read to your child.** Even if children are able to read themselves, they still enjoy hearing good stories read to them.

>> * **Read yourself!** And make sure your child knows you enjoy reading. There is nothing like a good role model.

>> * **Help your child attend special library programs.** Many children appreciate going with friends. Your child might like to be able to invite a friend or two to attend also.

• Activities, games, and arts and crafts that build reading skills and the enjoyment of reading.

We hope to see you at the library soon!

Sincerely,

Your Name
Title

TIP
A button making machine with parts and instructions can be ordered from Badge-A-Minit 348 North 30th Rd., Box 800 LaSalle, IL 61301 (815) 224-2090

INCENTIVE IDEAS

Many libraries give away prizes such as food coupons or paperback books as incentives for their reading clubs. Another idea is to present a button to each child who signs up for the reading club. Then, after a predetermined number of books have been read or an amount of time has been spent reading, the child can be given a wide ribbon to hang from the button. For every five books or thirty minutes in addition, the child is given a sticker to stick on the ribbon. Other ideas for incentives are coloring or game books, coupons, pencils, erasers, movie passes, teeshirts, and drawings for major prizes. A button design, reading log, certificate, and bookmark are also good ideas. If you decide to have a club type reading program, these items are used in the following way:

The children are given a reading log when they are signed up for the program to record time or titiles of books read. The children are also given a bookmark. After the children read a prescribed amount of time or number of books, they receive a button and certificate with their name on it.

DISPLAY IDEAS

Displays are always an excellent way to promote your reading club activities. Display some of these items with books from the bibliographies in each section.

1. *Camp Wanna-Read* Camping equipment, family items.
2. *Get Wild* nature items like shells, feathers, leaves, pinecones.
3. *Munchabunch* kitchen and cooking items like spoons, colorful mitts, apples, etc.
4. *Discover the Library* microscope, science materials, magnifying glass.

CONTINUING PROGRAMS

Here are two programs to keep kids returning to the library.

Secret Storyteller: Invite a parent or sibling of a reading club member to come and read or tell a story during your programs. Invite different people each week and keep their identity a secret. Let the children try to guess who the secret storyteller is.

Family Reading Club: Get as many members of the families of the children who sign up for the reading club to read 10 books over the course of 10 weeks like the kids. Make special "Family of Readers" certificates for those families who participate in this team effort.

RESOURCES FOR PROGRAMMING IDEAS:

Bauer, Carolyn Feller. *This Way to Books*. HW Wilson, 1983.

Carlson, Bernice Wells. *Let's Find the Big Idea: Fable and Story Skits to Dramatize*. Abingdon, 1982.

Gillespe, John T. and Corinne Naden. *Juniorplots*. Bowker, 1987.

Kohl, MaryAnn F. *Mudworks: Creative Clay, Dough, And Modeling Experiences*. Bright Ring, 1989,

Lima, Carolyn and John Lima. *A to Zoo: Subject Access to Children's Picture Books*. Bowker, 1989, 3rd Edition.

Lynn, Ruth. *Fantasy Literature for Children and Young Adults*. Bowker, 1989.

MacDonald, Margaret Read. *Booksharing: 101 Programs to Use With Preschoolers*. Library Professional Publications, 1988.

———. *Twenty Tellable Tales*. HW Wilson, 1986.

Painter, William. *Musical Story Hours*. Library Professional Publications, 1989.

SELECT BIBLIOGRAPHY

PRESCHOOL—GRADE 2

Afanasyev, Alexander. *The Fool and the Fish: A Tale From Russia*. Dial, 1990.

Everyone says Ivan is a lazy fool even when he finds a magic fish.

Alexander, Ellen. *The Llama and the Great Flood*. Thomas Y. Crowell, 1989.

A llama in Peru warns people of an impending flood.

Asch, Frank. *Monkey Face*. Parents Magazine Press, 1977.

Monkey draws a picture of his mother and adds to it using the advice of his animal friends.

Bach, Alice. *The Most Delicious Camping Trip Ever*. Harper & Row, 1976.

Two bears and Aunt Bear prepare for an unexpectedly enjoyable camping trip.

Barbour, Karen. *Little Nino's Pizzeria*. Harper & Row, 1987.

Tony's father's business becomes too big for Tony to help.

Brisson, Pat. *Your Best Friend Kate*. Bradbury, 1989.

Kate chronicles her family vacation in letters to her best friend at home.

Brunhoff, Jean de. *The Travels of Babar*. Random House, 1934.

An oversize book about the balloon adventures of a favorite elephant.

Calhoun, Mary. *Hot Air Henry*. Morrow, 1981.

A Siamese cat named Henry sneaks into a hot air balloon and is set aloft.

Carle, Eric. *The Grouchy Ladybug*. Crowell, 1977.

This ladybug challenges everyone to fights.

Caseley, Judith. *Apple Pie and Onions.* Greenwillow, 1987.

> Grandma's apple pie helps Rebecca to understand why grandma speaks Yiddish.

Cauley, Lorinda. *The Pancake Boy: An Old Norwegian Folk Tale.* Putnam, 1988.

> A variation on the gingerbread boy tale.

Cendrars, Blaise. *Shadows.* Scribners, 1982.

> A Caldecott winner explores the world of shadows.

Cocca-Leffler, Maryann. *Wednesday is Spaghetti Day.* Scholastic, 1989.

> On Wednesdays cat waits for its owners to leave to have a spaghetti party.

Coleridge, Ann. *The Friends of Emily Culpepper.* Putnam, 1987.

> Emily Culpepper takes very good care of her very small friends, whom she keeps in jars.

Delton, Judy. *My Mom Made Me Go To Camp.* Delacorte, 1989.

> After first disliking camp, the boy becomes a hero as well as learning to love it.

Demi. *Dragon Kites and Dragonflies.* Harcourt, Brace, Jovanovich, 1986.

> An illustrated collection of 22 Chinese nursery rhymes.

Donnelly, Liza. *Dinosaur Garden.* Scholastic, 1989.

> A boy plants a garden and it is soon filled with dinosaur friends.

Ehlert, Lois. *Color Zoo.* Lippincott, 1989.

> Basic shapes in bright colors are combined to make familar animals.

———. *Fish Eyes: A Book You Can Count On.* HBJ, 1990.

> A colorful counting book with a variety of fish.

Fleischman, Sid. *The Scarebird.* Greenwillow, 1988.

> A farmer helps out and befriends a headless scarecrow.

Galdone, Paul. *The Gingerbread Boy.* Seabury, 1975.

> Galdone's delightful retelling of the traditional tale.

Ginsburg, Mirra. *The Night It Rained Pancakes*. Greenwillow, 1980.

Ivan tricks his brother into not revealing the location of a pot of gold.

Goble, Paul. *Iktomi and the Boulder*. Orchard Watts, 1988.

Humorous adventures of Iktomi the trickster in several situations.

Gray, Nigel. *A Balloon for Grandad*. Orchard, 1988.

Father suggests that Sam's runaway balloon might be on a trip to Africa to visit grandad.

Gullikson, Sandy. *Trouble for Breakfast*. Dial, 1990.

Munchit and Crunchit the rabbit twins, Armadillo, Rufus Coyote, and Cousin Arnold all attempt to make a get well breakfast.

Henkes, Kevin. *Chester's Way*. Greenwillow, 1988.

Chester and Wilson do not want to be friends with the mouse girl Lilly.

Hines, Anna. *Daddy Makes the Best Spaghetti*. Clarion, 1986.

A father and son have a warm and helpful relationship as they cook together.

Hogrogian, Nonny. *Apple Tree! Apple Tree!* Children's, 1983.

A friendly apple tree gives gifts to some children, a bird, and a worm.

Hopkins, Lee Bennett. *Dinosaurs*. HBJ, 1987.

Various poems about giant reptiles.

Jenkin-Pearce, Suse. *The Enchanted Garden*. Oxford University Press, 1989.

The topiary animals in the garden come to life.

Kellogg, Steven. *Johnny Appleseed*. Morrow Junior Books, 1988.

The story of John Chapman who spreads good cheer and apple seeds.

Kemp, Anthea. *Mr. Percy's Magic Greenhouse*. Victor Gollancz, 1986.

Mr. Percy's magic words turn his greenhouse into a hot, steamy jungle.

Kerr, Judith. *The Tiger Who Came to Tea*. Coward McCann, 1969.

A tiger unexpectedly joins tea time.

Kimmell, Eric. *Anansi and the Moss Covered Rock.* Holiday House, 1988.

Anansi the spider uses a magic rock to steal the other animal's food.

King, Larry. *Because of Lozo Brown.* Viking Kesterl, 1988.

The narrator is very frightened of the new boy Lozo Brown, who turns out to be not so big or scary.

Kitchen, Burt. *Gorilla-Chinchilla.* Dial, 1990.

Rhyming verse about animal pairs.

Lester, Helen. *Pookins Gets Her Way.* Houghton Mifflin, 1987.

Pookins insists that an elf turn her into a flower.

Levinson, Ricki. *I Go With My Family to Grandma's.* Dutton, 1986.

Several children go and visit their grandmother in turn of the century New York.

Luenn, Nancy. *The Dragon Kite.* HBJ, 1982.

A crafty thief constructs a kite in order to steal the golden dolphins from the palace of the shogun.

Lopshire, Robert. *Put Me in the Zoo.* Random House, 1960.

The age old favorite about the creature with amazing spots.

McPhail, David. *Pig Pig Goes to Camp.* Dutton, 1983.

Pig Pig makes some unusual friends at camp.

Mahy, Margaret. *The Boy With Two Shadows.* Lippincott, 1987.

A boy is stuck with two shadows: his own and that of a witch.

Mahy, Margaret. *The Seven Chinese Brothers.* Scholastic, 1989.

A retelling of the classic tale about some brothers with a talent for avoiding death.

Moseley, Francis. *The Dinosaur Eggs.* Francis Barrons, 1988.

Alfred and Mary wish for children and find three dinosaur eggs which they adopt.

Narahashi, Keiko. *I Have a Friend.* M. K. McElderry, 1987.

A boy knows his shadow will return when the sun does.

Noble, Trinka Hankes. *The King's Tea.* Dial, 1979.

> Each character in this story blames the other for the sour milk in the king's tea.

Numeroff, Laura Joffe. *If You Give a Mouse a Cookie.* Harper & Row, 1985.

> A circular tale about a mouse who asks for various things.

Obligado, Lillian. *Faint Frogs Feeling Feverish.* Viking, 1983.

> The alphabet explained through tongue twisters.

O'Keefe, Susan Heyboer. *One Hungry Monster: A Counting Rhyme Book.* Little Brown, 1989.

> A band of hungry monsters raids the kitchen in this rhymed counting book.

Priceman, Marjorie. *Friend or Frog.* Houghton Mifflin, 1989.

> Kate's best friend Hilton the frog needs a new home.

Sadler, Marilyn. *Alistair Underwater.* Simon and Schuster, 1990.

> Alistair rescues his newfound sea creature friends.

Scheer, Julian. *Rain Makes Apple Sauce.* Holiday House, 1964.

> A series of silly statements and humorous illustrations.

Schulevitz, Uri. *One Monday Morning.* Scribner's, 1967.

> Royal visitors come for tea to a tenement on a rainy day.

Schwartz, Amy. *How I Captured a Dinosaur.* Orchard, 1988.

> Liz discovers a dinosaur while camping and takes it home.

Schwartz, Amy. *Oma and Bobo.* Bradbury, 1987.

> Alice's new dog Bobo does not get along with grandma.

Seuss, Dr. *Oh Say Can You Say!* Beginner Books, 1979.

> Tongue twisters about imaginary animals.

Slepian, Jan. *The Silly Listening Book.* Follett, 1967.

> Humorous rhymed book about all kinds of silly sound effects.

Taylor, Scott. *Dinosaur James.* Morrow Junior Books, 1990.

> James likes to pretend he is a dinosaur.

Tompert, Anne. *Nothing Sticks Like a Shadow.* Houghton Mifflin, 1984.

Rabbit tries to get rid of his shadow.

Van Allsburg, Chris. *Two Bad Ants.* Houghton Mifflin, 1988.

Two brave ants leave the comfort of their colony for the adventure of a human kitchen.

Van Laan, Nancy. *Rainbow Crow: A Lenape Tale.* Alfred A. Knopf, 1989.

How crow brought fire to the earth.

Wescott, Nadine. *The Lady with the Alligator Purse.* Joy Street Books, 1988.

The traditional jump rope rhyme in picture book form.

Wildsmith, Brian. *Bear's Adventure.* Pantheon, 1981.

Bear accidentally becomes part of a parade.

Willard, Nancy. *The Well Mannered Balloon.* Harcourt Brace World, 1979.

A balloon with a pirate face comes to life and is very rude.

Williams, Vera. *Stringbean's Trip to the Shining Sea.* Greenwillow, 1987.

A story told in postcards of a journey from Kansas to the West Coast.

Wilson, Sarah. *Muskrat, Muskrat, Eat Your Peas!* Simon & Schuster, 1989.

The smallest muskrat finally doesn't have to eat peas, but spaghetti instead.

Yorinks, Arthur. *Louis the Fish.* Farrar, 1980.

An unhappy man becomes a very happy fish.

GRADES 3 AND UP

Adler, C.S. *Always and Forever Friends.* Ticknor & Fields, 1988.

Eleven-year-old Wendy is having trouble making friends until she meets Honor and they become friends.

Adoff, Arnold. *Chocolate Dreams.* Lothrop, 1989.

A collection of chocolate poems.

Alcock, Vivan. *The Monster Garden.* Delacorte, 1988.

Frankie uses some material from her father's lab in her terrarium and accidentally makes Monnie, a monster.

———. *The Sylvia Game.* Delacorte, 1984.

Emily bears a striking resemblance to a famous portrait of long dead Sylvia, owned by some neighbors.

Ancona, George. *Handtalk Zoo.* Four Winds, 1989.

The signs for various zoo animals are shown in photographs.

Arnold, Caroline. *Dinosaur Mountain: Graveyard of the Past.* Clarion, 1990.

A visit to dinosaur monument quarry in Utah.

Arnosky, Jim. *Crinkleroot's Guide to Walking in Wild Places.* Bradbury, 1990.

A guide to the outdoors, including listening, looking, and deciphering nature's clues.

———. *Crinkleroot's Guide to Animal Tracks and Wildlife Signs.* Putnam, 1979.

A folksy hero leads us on a trek through the woods.

Ashabranner, Brent. *People Who Make A Difference.* Cobble Hill, 1989.

Chapters on everyday heroes such as scientists and policemen.

Auch, Mary Jane. *Mom is Dating Weird Wayne.* Holiday House, 1988.

Jenna dislikes Weird Wayne the weatherman whom her mother is dating.

Bjork, Christina. *Linnea in Monet's Garden.* R & S Books, 1987.

A young French girl learns about gardening and Monet.

———. *Linnea's Windowsill Garden.* Farrar, Straus & Giroux, 1987.

Readers get a tour of Linnea's small garden.

Booth, Jerry. *The Beast Book.* Little Brown, 1988.

A brown paper school book filled with fun ideas, facts, and activities about dinosaurs.

Bulla, Clyde Robert. *The Chalk Box Kid.* Random House, 1987.

Gregory draws a wonderful garden in an old burned out house.

Byars, Betsy. *A Blossom Promise.* Delacorte, 1987.

> The Blossom family, including grandpa, cope with life after a flood in Anderson County.

Catling, Patrick. *The Chocolate Touch.* Morrow, 1979.

> A retelling of the King Midas story with a chocolate twist.

Chetwin, Grace. *Out of the Dark World.* Lothrop, Lee, and Shepherd, 1985.

> While toying with their father's computer, Meg and Sue discover a boy's mind trapped inside.

Cleary, Beverly. *Dear Mr. Henshaw.* ABC-Clio, 1987.

> A boy pours out his problems in letters to his favorite author.

Clifford, Eth. *The Remembering Box.* Houghton Mifflin, 1985

> Nine-year-old Joshua's weekly visits to his grandmother to listen to her stories help him accept his family, its traditions, and finally grandmother's death.

Conford, Ellen. *Hail, Hail Camp Timberwood.* Little Brown, 1978.

> Thirteen-year-old Melanie's first camp.

————. *What's Cooking, Jenny Archer?* Little Brown, 1990.

> Another in the Jenny Archer series about cooking.

Conrad, Pam. *Stonewords.* Harper and Row, 1990.

> A friendship develops between Zoe and Zoe Louise, girls who live in different centuries.

Danzinger, Paula. *There's a Bat in Bunk Five.* Delacorte, 1980.

> A sequel to *The Cat Ate My Gymsuit.*

DeClements, Barthe. *Five Finger Discount.* Delacorte, 1989.

> Can Jerry, whose father is in prison for stealing, be friends with Grace, the daughter of a preacher?

Delton, Judy. *Cookies and Crutches.* Dell, 1988.

> Molly finds out that cooking is not as easy as it seems.

D'Ignazio, Fred. *Chip Mitchell and the Case of the Chocolate Covered Bugs.* Dutton, 1985.

Ten mini-mysteries featuring Chip Mitchell the computer wizard.

Elish, Dan. *The Worldwide Dessert Contest.* Orchard, 1988.

John Applefeller dreams of winning the worldwide dessert contest.

Etra, Jonathan. *Aliens For Breakfast.* Random House, 1988.

Richard finds an alien in his cereal box.

Gackenbach, Dick. *Timid Timothy's Tongue Twisters.* Holiday House, 1986.

Silly tongue twisters for young children.

Gormley, Beatrice. *Wanted: UFO.* Dutton, 1990.

Elise and Nick love outer space for different reasons, until they encounter alien beings.

Gray, Genevieve. *A Kite for Benny.* McGraw Hill, 1972.

Benny is a poor boy determined to have his very own kite.

Hahn, Mary Downing. *Daphne's Book.* Clarion, 1983.

A friendship between two very different girls.

———. *The Doll in the Garden.* Clarion, 1989.

A grouchy older lady and a hidden antique doll lead Ashley on a time-travel adventure.

Hayes, Mary. *Wordchanger.* Lothrop, Lee, and Shepherd, 1983.

William discovers his stepfather has created a machine that can change the words in books and thus the outcomes of the stories and history.

Howe, James. *Hot Fudge.* Morrow, 1989.

Someone steals the latest batch of the Monroe family's chewy chocolate fudge.

Issacson, Philip. *Round Buildings, Square Buildings, Buildings That Wiggle Like a Fish.* Knopf, 1988.

A straightforward exploration of architectural styles and their beauty.

Kline, Suzy. *Orp and the Chop Suey Burgers.* Putnam, 1990.

Orp enters a recipe contest and must compete against cooks from all over.

Landon, Lucinda. *Meg MacIntosh and the Mystery at Camp Creepy.* Joy Street Books, 1990.

The versatile girl detective solves a camp mystery.

Landsman, Sandy. *The Gadget Factor.* Atheneum, 1984.

Two teenage geniuses build a computer universe and are surprised when its laws of time travel work in the real world also.

Leverich, Kathleen. *Best Enemies.* Greenwillow, 1989.

The only thing worse than being Felicity Doll's enemy for Priscilla is being her best friend.

Litchfield, Ada. *Words in Our Hands.* Whitman, 1980.

Michael's life with his deaf parents is described.

Little, Jean. *Hey World, Here I Am.* Harper & Row, 1986.

A collection of poems on being yourself.

Livingston, Myra Cohn. *I Like You If You Like Me.* Margaret K. McElderry, 1987.

Short poems on friendship from various sources and time periods.

Macaulay, David. *The Way Things Work.* Houghton Mifflin, 1988.

Humorous explanations of the history of inventions and machine engineering.

MacDonald, Margaret Read. *When the Lights Go Out: Twenty Scary Stories to Tell.* HW Wilson, 1988.

Twenty scary folktales to tell with notes on stories and techniques.

McKenna, Colleen Shaunessy. *Too Many Murphys.* Scholastic, 1988.

Third-grader Collette sometimes gets tired of taking care of her three younger siblings.

Mayne, William. *Gideon Ahoy.* Delacorte, 1989.

Gideon, the deaf and brain damaged brother of 12-year-old Eva, gets a job opening locks in the canal.

Murie, Johan Olaus. *Field Guide to Animal Tracks*. Houghton Mifflin, 1975.

Straightforward guide to detecting and identifying animal tracks.

Naylor, Phyllis Reynolds. *Beetles Lightly Toasted*. Atheneum, 1987.

Andy must prove that his essay premised on eating beetles is true.

Nixon, Joan Lowry. *Maggie, Too*. HBJ, 1985.

Maggie is banished to the crazy household of a grandmother she does not know, because of her producer father's upcoming remarriage.

Pellowski, Anne. *Hidden Stories in Plants*. Macmillan, 1990

Easy to tell stories about plants and activities to go with them.

Pfeffer, Susan Beth. *Dear Dad, Love Laurie*. Scholastic, 1989.

Laurie writes once a week to her dad who lives 1,000 miles away.

———. *Rewind to Yesterday*. Delacorte, 1988.

———. *Future Forward*. Delacorte, 1989.

Kelly and Scott Forrest use a VCR to travel forward and backward in time in these companion books.

Pinkwater, Daniel. *Fat Men From Space*. Dodd Mead, 1977.

William encounters aliens who love junk food.

Pryor, Bonnie. *Vinegar, Pancakes, and Vanishing Cream*. Morrow, 1987.

The ups and downs of the life of Martin Elwood Snodgrass.

Raskin, Ellen. *The Westing Game*. Dutton, 1978.

A convoluted mystery involving deciphering a will.

Riskind, Mary. *Apple is My Sign*. Houghton Mifflin, 1981.

A deaf boy is sent to a residential school for the first time in the 1900s.

Rocklin, Joanne. *Dear Baby*. Collier Macmillan, 1988.

An 11-year-old adjusts to life with a new baby in the house.

San Souci, Robert. *Short and Shivery: Thirty Chilling Tales*. Doubleday, 1987.

Thirty short, spooky tales from Russia, Virginia, Ireland, and various other parts of the world.

Sant, Thomas. *The Amazing Adventures of Albert and His Flying Machine.* Dutton Lodestar, 1990.

Albert Halperin inherits a thousand dollars and tries to make himself a zephycar, a personal hovercraft.

Saunders, Susan. *The Daring Rescue of Marlon the Swimming Pig.* Random House, 1987.

Marlon's friends try to save the 300-pound trick pig from becoming bacon.

Schneider, Susan. *Please Send Junk Food.* Putnam, 1985.

All you will need to know about going to camp no matter what kind of camper you are.

Schwartz, Alvin. *Scary Stories to Tell in the Dark.* Lippincott, 1981.

Ghost stories collected from American folklore.

———. *A Twister of Twists, A Tangler of Tongues.* Lippincott, 1972.

Tongue twisters from various languages.

Schwartz, David. *The Hidden Life of the Pond.* Crown, 1988.

Animals and plants that live in a pond.

Sleator, William. *Interstellar Pig.* Dutton, 1984.

At first Barney enjoys the weird game his strange new neighbors play that involves a plastic pink pig, but he gradually comes to suspect there is more to the game than he first thought.

Slote, Alfred. *The Trading Game.* J.B. Lippincott, 1990.

Baseball cards are important, but to this boy's grandfather the actual game is what he lives for.

Smith, Robert K. *Chocolate Fever.* Dell, 1979.

Henry gets the first recorded case of chocolate fever.

Steiner, Barbara. *Oliver Dibbs and the Dinosaur Cause.* FourWinds, 1986.

Oliver attempts to adopt a dinosaur as a state symbol.

Strauss, Linda. *The Alexandra Ingredient.* Crown, 1988.

When Alexandra adopts Mike Potts in the adopt-a-grandparent program, she is not prepared for the many problems that follow.

Van Allsburg, Chris. *The Garden of Abdul Gasazi.* Houghton Mifflin, 1979.

Allen chases a dog into the garden of a retired magician.

———. *Jumanji.* Houghton Mifflin, 1981.

When two children play a game they have found the events in the game begin to actually happen.

Van Leeuwen, Jean. *Dear Mom, You're Ruining My Life.* Dial, 1989.

Samantha communicates to her mom who is an embarassment to her, as well as to the tooth fairy.

Yolen, Jane. *Things That Go Bump in the Night.* Harper & Row, 1989.

A collection of original chillers by authors such as Yolen, William Sleator, Bruce Coville, and Diana Wynne Jones.

FILMOGRAPHY

The Amazing Bone. Weston Woods, 1985, 11 min.

> Pearl the pig happens upon a magical bone that uses its tricks to save her from perilous situations. From the book by William Steig. (K)

Amazing Cosmic Awareness of Duffy Moon. Time Life Films. 1972, 32 min.

> Duffy is a "Shrimp" who develops other powers to meet his challenges. (I-J)

Animals Nobody Loved. National Geographic, 1975, 52 min.

> National Geographic special about misunderstood animals, including the coyotye. (G)

Burt Dow: Deep Water Man. Weston Woods, 1973, 10 min.

> Burt Dow, a retired seaman, sets sail again and hitches a ride with a whale. (K)

Curious George. Churchill, 1984, 14 min.

> Curious George is brought to the city by the man in the yellow hat and eventually ends up on an unplanned balloon ride. From the book by H.A. Rey. (K)

Danny and the Dinosaur. Weston Woods, 1990, 9 min.

> A video presentation of the book by Syd Hoff. (K-I)

Dinosaur. Pyramid Films and Video, 1980, 14 min.

> Claymation fantasy about a fifth grader's report on dinosaurs. (G)

The Doughnuts. Weston Woods, 1964, 26 min.

> A doughnut machine goes berserk and leaves Homer Price up to his ears in doughnuts. From the book by Robert McKloskey. (K-I)

Drummer Hoff. Weston Woods, 1969, 6 min.

> Based on the book by Ed Emberley, a repetitive rhyme about the firing of a cannon.(K)

The Electric Grandmother. Learning Corporation of America, 1982, 34 min.

Based on the Ray Bradbury short story about a magical grandmother who brings love to a motherless household. (I)

The Emperor's Oblong Pancake. Sterling, 1963, 6 min.

Retelling of the book by Peter Hughes about an emperor who wants all of the round items in his kingdom to become oblong. (K)

A Firefly Named Torchy. Guidance Associates. 1972, 8 min.

Based on the book by Bernard Waber. About a firefly whose light shines too brightly. (K-I)

Fish is Fish. Distribution 16, 1985, 5 min.

When a tadpole changes into a frog, is it still a fish? Based on the book by Leo Lionni. (K)

The Fisherman and His Wife. Weston Woods, 1970, 20 min.

Shadow puppet rendition of the traditional folk tale about a magic fish. (K-I)

Foolish Frog. Weston Woods, 1971, 8 min.

A film version of the Pete Seeger song about a frog who puffs up with pride.(K-I)

Frog and Toad are Friends. Churchill, 1985, 18 min.

Arnold Lobel's characters come to life in five claymation episodes. (K-I)

The Ghost of Thomas Kempe. MTI Teleprograms, 1979, 48 min.

Adapted from the Penelope Lively novel about James, who accidentally releases a ghost from an antique bottle. (I)

How to Be a Perfect Person in Just Three Days. Learning Corporation of America, 1985, 55 min.

Milo Crimpy's life is a disaster until he meets up with Dr. K. Pinkerton Silverfish. Based on the book by Stephen Manes. (I-H)

If I Ran the Zoo. Filmstrip or VHS, Communication Skills, Inc. 7 min, 1978.

Iconographic treatment of a favorite Dr. Seuss tale. (K)

In the Night Kitchen. Weston Woods, 1987, 6 min.

Mickey is awakened by three funny bakers who try to bake him in a cake. Based on the book by Maurice Sendak.(K)

The Legend of Johnny Appleseed. 20 minutes, 1966, Demco.

An exaggerated tale about the loveable hero John Chapman. (K-J)

The Letter. Films Incorporated, 1970, 5 min.

Follows the trail of a red-enveloped letter from mailbox to post office to destination. (K-I)

A Letter to Amy. Weston Woods, 1970, 7 min.

Based on the book by Ezra Jack Keats. Peter writes a very special birthday invitation. (K)

Mole as Watchmaker. Phoenix, 1976, 6 min.

At first Mole fights with the cuckoo from the clock but eventually makes friends. (K-I)

The Napping House. Weston Woods, 1985, 5 min.

Sleeping creatures, including a grandmother, pile up in the Napping House. (K)

The New Friend. Made to Order Library Productions, 1981, 11 min.

Howard the mallard duck and an unlikely crew of friends depend on each other one winter for survival. Based on the book *Howard* by James Stephenson. (K-I)

Pedro. Walt Disney, 1943, 5 min.

Pedro the airplane gets a chance to deliver the mail against some tough odds. (K)

Philly Philodendron. Films Incorporated, 1973, 12 min.

A humorous tale about a boy growing a plant told from the philodendron's point of view. (I)

Ramona's Bad Day. Churchill, 1988, 27 min.

Everything goes wrong for Ramona. Based on the Beverly Cleary book *Ramona.* (K-I)

Runaway Ralph. Chuchill, 1987, 40 min.

Ralph S. Mouse roars to camp on his little red motorcycle. Based on the Beverly Cleary book. (K-I)

The Runt of the Litter. Films Incorporated, 1976, 13 min.

> Wilbur the runt pig feels lonely until Charlotte, a beautiful spider, befriends him. Based on *Charlotte's Web* by E.B. White. (K-J)

Sea Dream. Phoenix, 1980, 6 min.

> A little girl does various activities with her octopus friend, including having tea. (K-I)

The Sound Collector. National Film Board of Canada, 1982, 12min.

> Leonard is a 6 year old who collects sounds and turns them into fabulous stories. (K-I)

Strega Nona. Weston Woods, 1977, 9 min.

> Strega Nona leaves Big Anthony in charge of her magic pasta pot with disastrous results. Based on the book by Tomie DePaola. (K-I)

Swimmy. Conn Films, Incorporated, 1969, 6 min.

> Based on the book by Leo Lionni. A small black fish outwits a great tuna.(K-I)

Watch Out for My Plant. Barr Films, 1972, 14 min.

> A young inner-city boy plants a flower in a small patch of ground. (K-J)

PATTERN APPENDIX

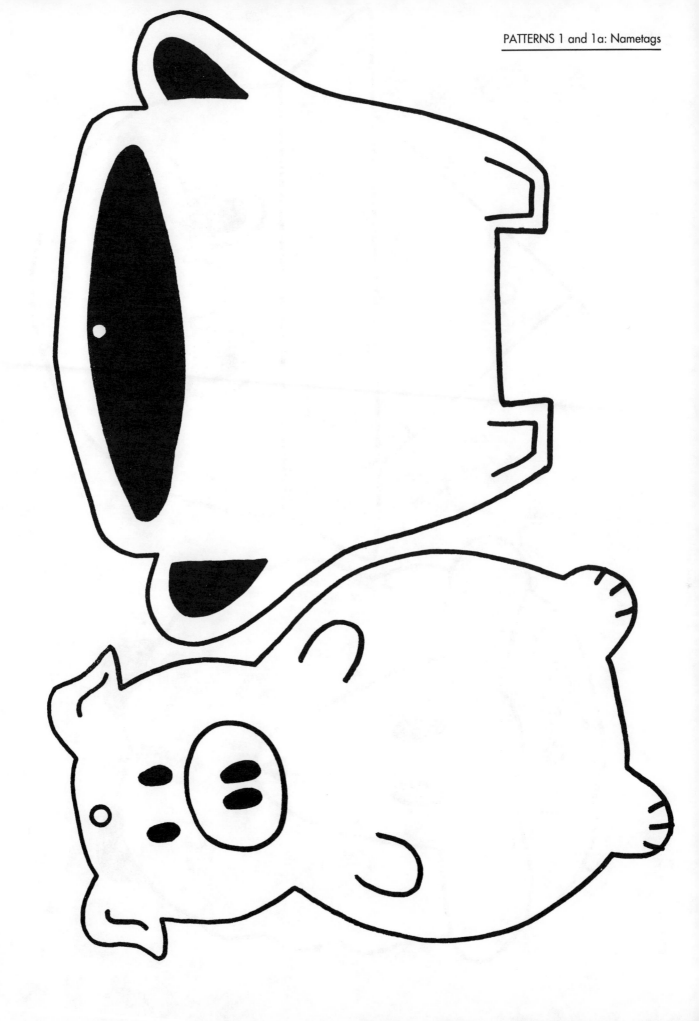

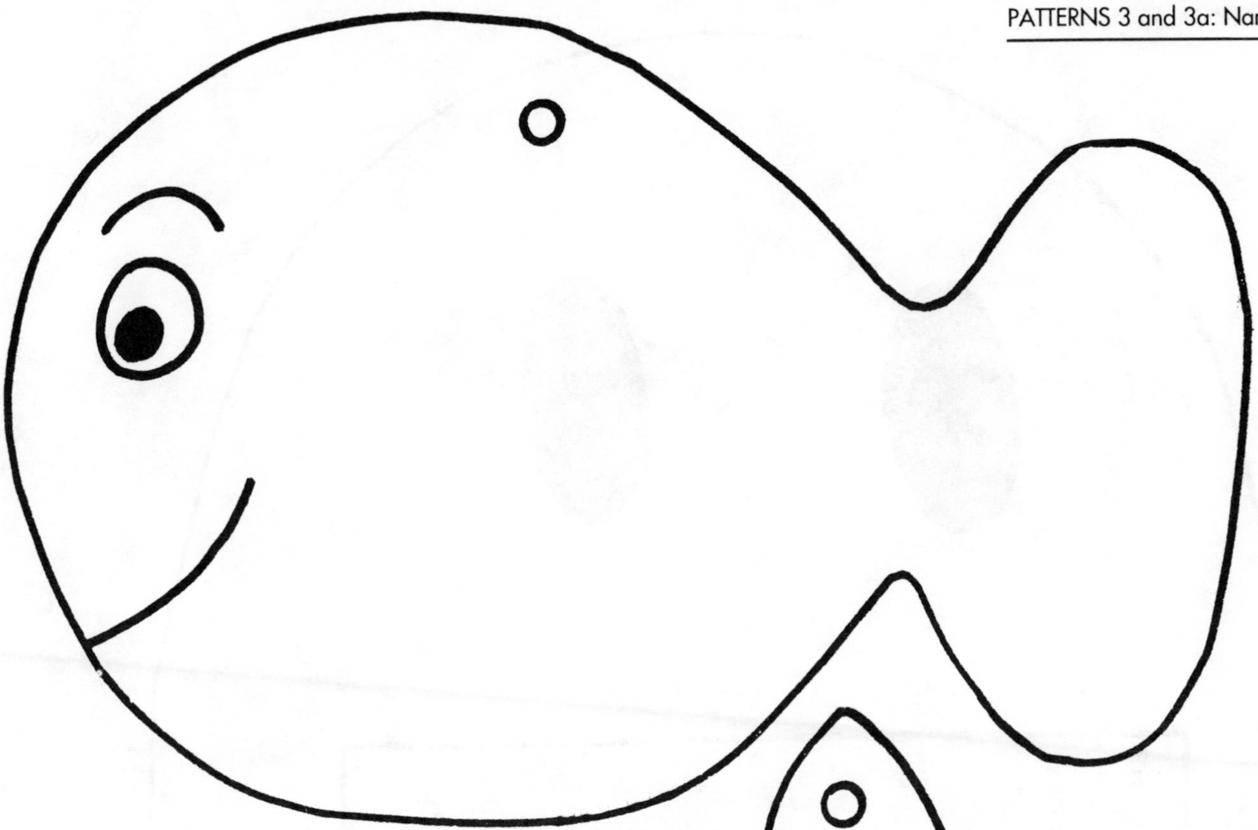

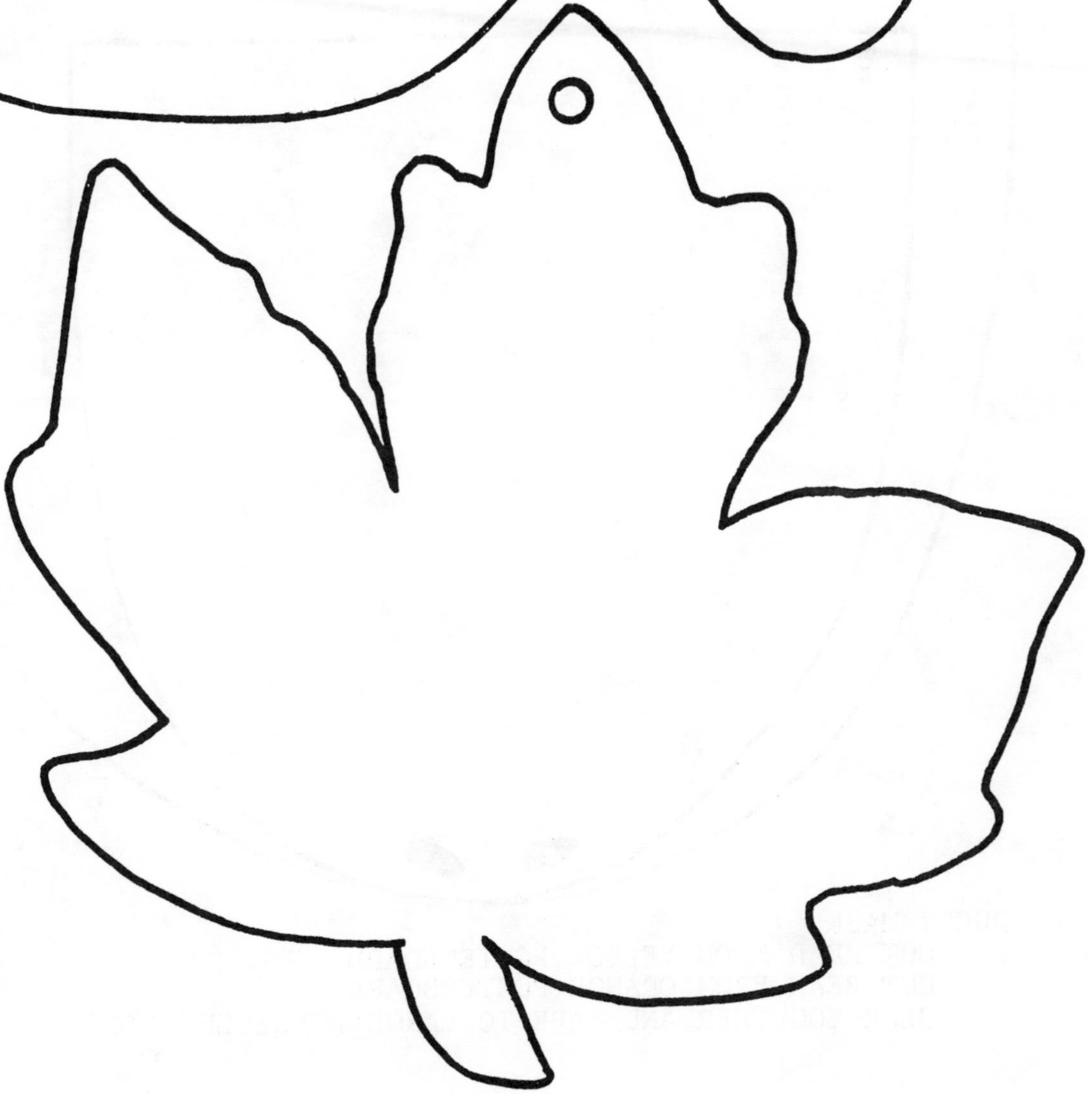

DUCKY MASK
1. CUT HEAD FROM YELLOW POSTERBOARD.
2. CUT BEAK FROM ORANGE POSTERBOARD.
3. GLUE TOGETHER AND TAPE TO LARGE POPSICLE STICK.

ILY PUPPET

COPY ONTO STIFF PAPER.
CUT OUT AND TAPE TO POPSICLE STICK.

LUNCH SACK PIGS

CUT FOUR LEGS, TWO EARS, ONE NOSE,
AND ONE TAIL FROM PINK PAPER.

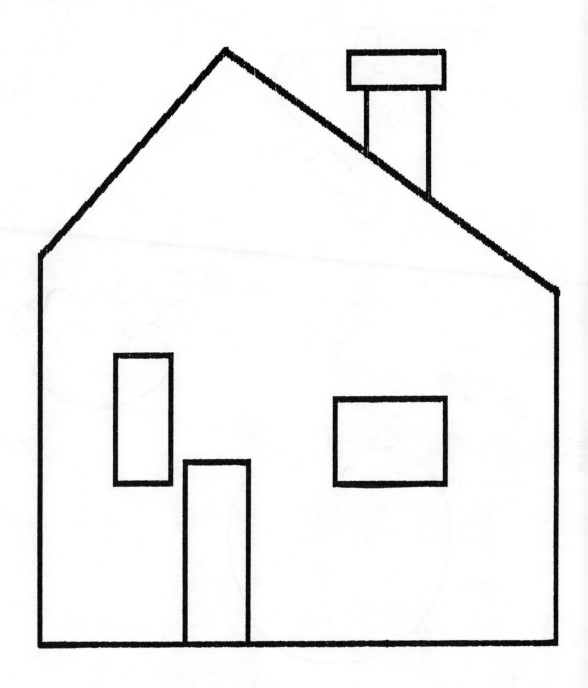

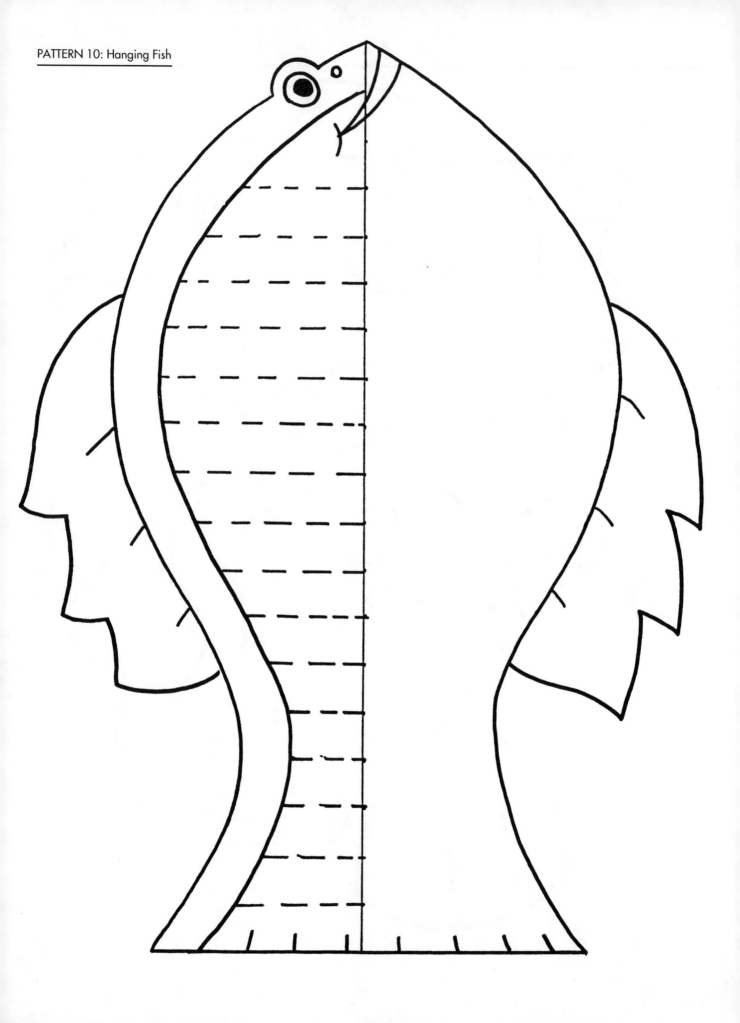

PATTERN 10: Hanging Fish

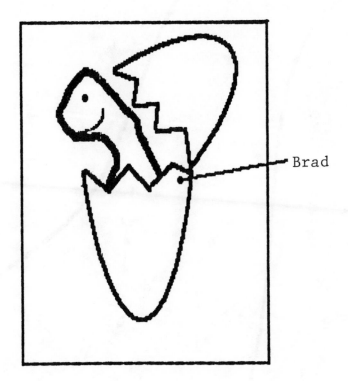

Brad

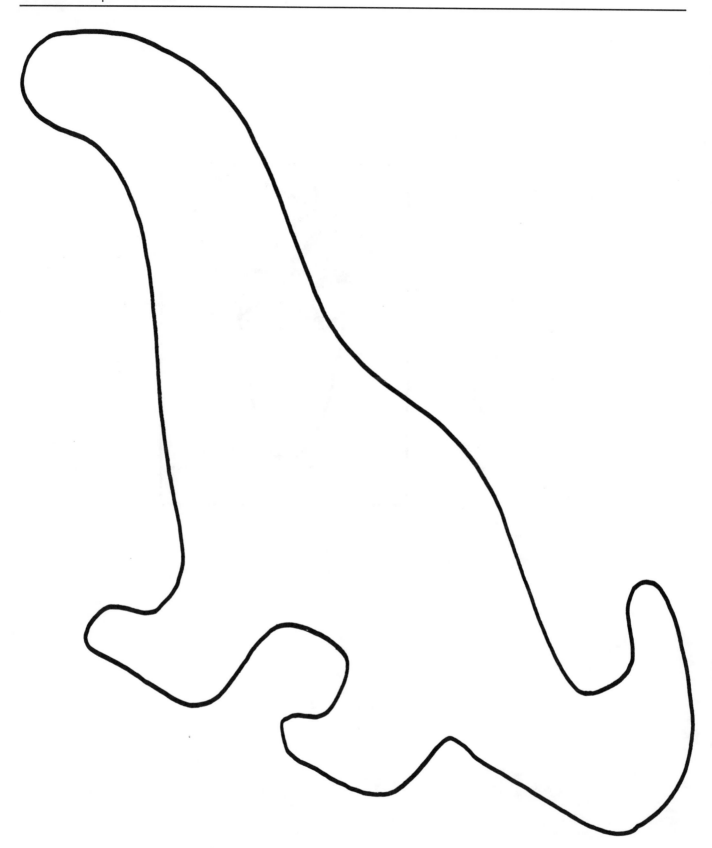

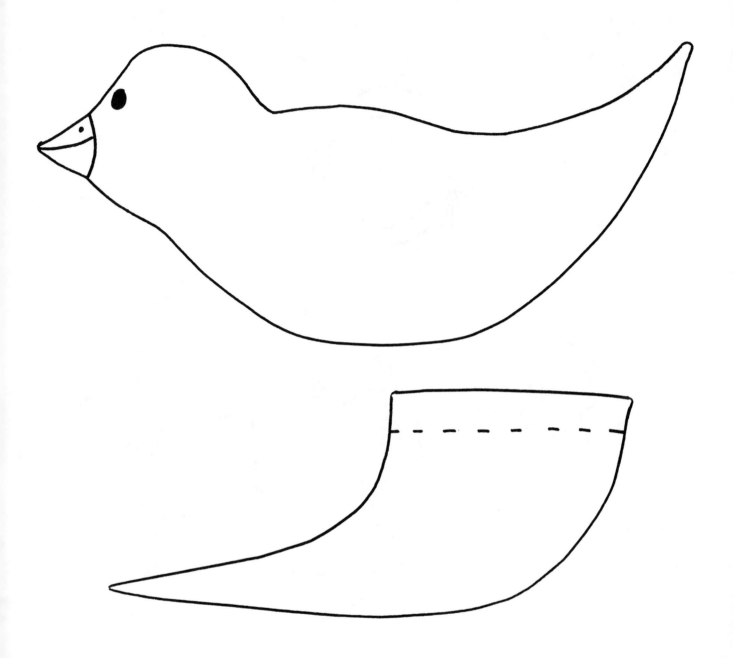

CUT ONE BODY AND TWO WINGS

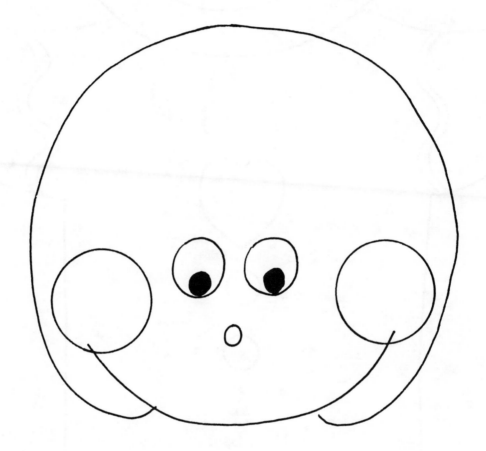

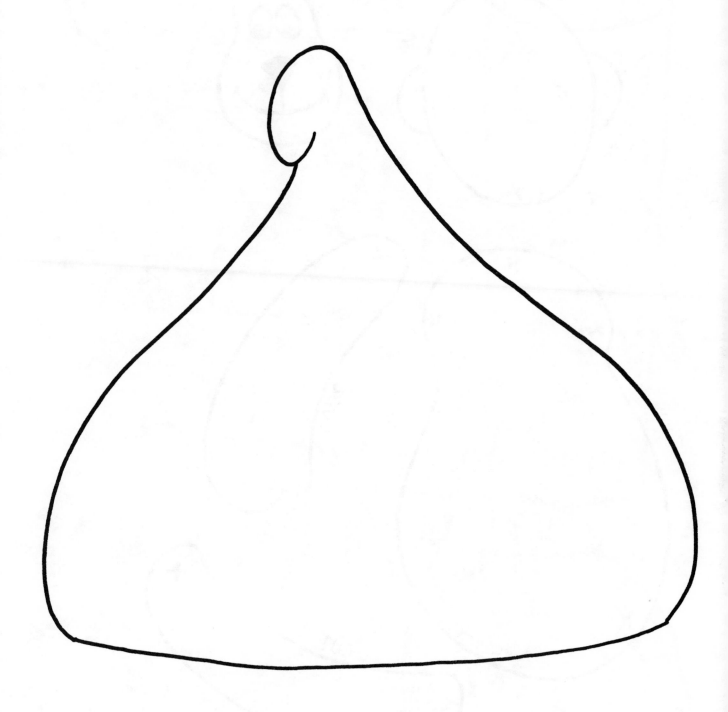

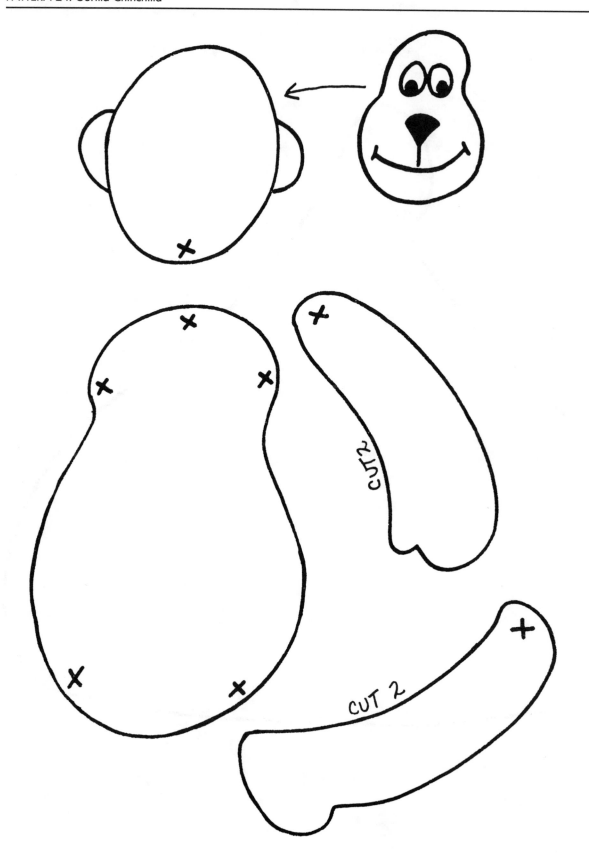

CUT 2

CUT 2

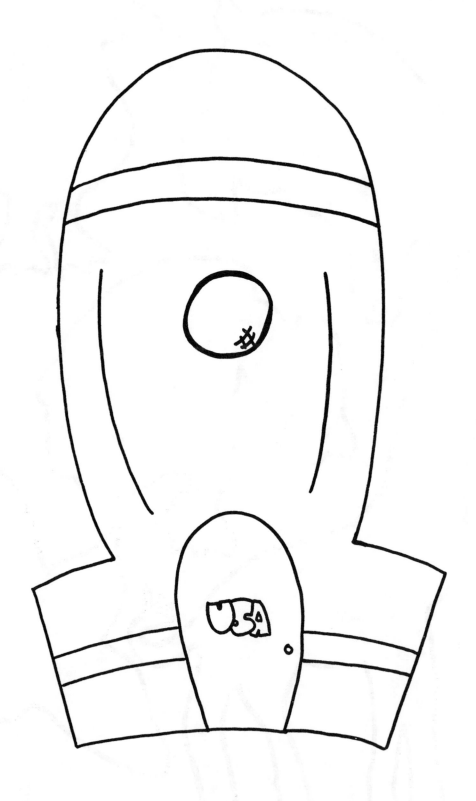

INDEX

Robin Works is Youth Services Librarian at the Hurst Public Library in Texas. She was previously with the Children's Department of the Richardson Public Library in Richardson, Texas.

Dr. Barbara L. Stein is Associate Professor at the School of Library and Information Science at the University of North Texas. She has experience both as a school teacher and a media specialist.

Typography: C. Roberts Typesetting
Cover: Apicella Design